Intellectual Well-Being Workbook

Facilitator Reproducible Sessions for Motivated Behavior Modification

John J. Liptak, Ed.D.
Ester R.A. Leutenberg

Duluth, Minnesota

Whole Person
101 W. 2nd St., Suite 203
Duluth, MN 55802

800-247-6789

books@wholeperson.com
www.wholeperson.com

Intellectual Well-Being Workbook
Facilitator Reproducible Sessions
for Motivated Behavior Modification

Printed in the United States of America

10 9 8 7 6 5 4 3 2 1

Editorial Director: Carlene Sippola
Art Director: Joy Morgan Dey

Library of Congress Control Number: 2014909584
ISBN: 978-1-57025-316-4

Our thanks to these professionals who make us look good!

Art Director – Joy Dey
Editor and Lifelong Teacher – Eileen Regen
Editorial Director – Carlene Sippola
Proofreader – Jay Leutenberg
Reviewer – Carol Butler

Introduction for the Facilitator

What is Intellectual Well-Being?

Overall well-being and a life free from major sources of stress have many dimensions. Intellectual well-being is important to a sense of overall wellness. The intellectual dimension of wellness, although often overlooked and undervalued, is extremely important in coping with stress and living a fulfilling life. Intellectual well-being can be difficult to describe, but it is essentially related to how interested your clients are in learning new skills, expanding their knowledge, thinking critically, seeking out new and interesting challenges, maintaining a sense of creativity and curiosity, searching for lifelong learning opportunities and stimulating mental activities, and being open to new ideas. If your clients are not exhibiting these characteristics, they may need to develop more effective intellectual wellness habits. When clients begin developing intellectual well-being habits, they begin to exhibit greater participation in creative, scholastic, cultural and community-based activities.

The *Intellectual Well-Being Workbook* is designed to help your clients enhance existing intellectual wellness traits and develop new attitudes that will improve their intellectual health. By completing the assessments, activities and exercises, you will help your clients to achieve the following

- Begin engaging in clear thinking and recall with minimal interference from emotional baggage
- Think independently rather than blindly going with the thinking of the crowd
- Think critically about local, community, national and international issues
- Use effective reasoning skills
- Maintain an open mind to new situations and novel approaches
- Develop and broaden understanding and acceptance of their cultural heritage
- Apply what they have learned at home or on a job
- Pick up easily on new concepts and ideas
- Develop an appreciation and enthusiasm for lifelong learning
- Develop an interest in engaging in intellectually stimulating activities throughout their lifespan
- Utilize their accumulated knowledge and experience for the greater good.

Living an intellectually healthy existence sounds easy, but is often very difficult to accomplish in everyday life. Many people experience stress in their lives when they are faced with new situations, exposed to people who are different from themselves, and frightened by new ideas and novel ways to approach situations in their lives. Intellectually well people find that they are able to approach new ideas and situations with enthusiasm and are not restricted to only that which has been done before. They are creative and always looking for ways to improve themselves and their future. They are curious and approach life with passionate desire to understand and embrace opportunities to learn new things. They will have the tools and techniques to cope with difficult life situations through being open-minded, able to pick up on new ideas, and interested in improving themselves. The *Intellectual Well-Being Workbook* is designed to help your clients understand how the many ways intellectual well-being can reduce stress and enhance their overall life satisfaction.

Intellectual Well-Being Workbook Sections

Observable actions and mannerisms that people display when reacting to life events are called behaviors. Behavior modification involves identifying ineffective behaviors, intentionally targeting them, setting goals for behavioral change, monitoring progress and determining effective rewards for improved behaviors.

The *Mind-Body Wellness Series* is composed of workbooks designed to help people learn how to discontinue old, destructive health habits and adopt new, healthy lifestyle choices. The model, referred to as Motivated Behavior Modification (MBM), looks at specific learned behaviors and the impact of environmental stimuli on those behaviors. It focuses on helping participants change undesirable and unhealthy lifestyle behaviors by objectively identifying unrealistic behaviors and replacing them with healthier, more effective behaviors.

Section 1 – Open to New Ideas – This section will help participants explore how open they are to new ways of thinking and new ideas.

Section 2 – Lifelong Learning – This section will help participants explore how motivated and interested they are to engage in learning both in the classroom and outside of the classroom.

Section 3 – Thinking Skills – This section will help participants explore their mental functions including information processing, flexibility in thinking, and application of use of thinking skills to regulate emotions.

Section 4 – Creativity Thinking – This section will help participants explore how well they can visualize, experience and express their creativity.

Section 5 – Critical Thinking – This section will help participants explore how well they question what they read and hear, create new ideas, use information to solve problems and make decisions in life.

Section 6 – Mental Sharpness – This section will help participants explore how well they remember things, focus their attention and concentrate when needed, and make good judgments.

Section 7 – Independent Thinking – This section helps participants explore how well they can evaluate information for decision making and make effective decisions with that information.

(Continued on the next page)

Changing Unhealthy Behaviors

Developing healthy mental functioning can be difficult, as implied in the adage "It's hard to teach an old dog new tricks!" Intellectual well-being brings a sense of life satisfaction, joy and contentment. However, most people must work to develop healthy mental functions and that is what this workbook does. This can be a challenging task for participants, but they can successfully change unhealthy thinking to healthier thinking. This workbook uses a model known as MBM (Motivated Behavior Modification). For participants to be successful, you as the facilitator can enhance their motivation in several ways.

Components of Each MBM Section

1. SELF-ASSESSMENT
Step 1 is the self-assessment of participants' current level of intellectual well-being. Encourage participants to take one step at a time. By working on one set of behaviors at a time, the task of changing behaviors will not feel insurmountable. Because mental functioning can be difficult to enhance, it is important that they take small steps and work slowly to change how their thinking affects their lives. By trying to change more than one mental function at a time, people set themselves up for failure. Encourage participants to keep it simple! Each section is set up in a step format for the MBM of the intellectual functioning and wellness of each participant.

2. SUPPORT SYSTEM
Step 2 will guide participants to develop a support system of people who can help them achieve their goals of intellectual well-being. Encourage participants to develop a support system to help them be more aware of the importance of mental functioning in their lives. It is important that you encourage participants to define who in their lives can help and support them while they learn to develop their intellectual abilities to function more effectively. Encourage participants to develop a support system so that they can engage their minds in lively interactions with the world around them. Explain that each participant's support system will vary for each type of behavior.

3. JOURNALING
Step 3 includes responses to journaling questions to help participants reflect about their current and past mental functioning. Encourage participants to write everything down in their journals. Remind them that words are shallow and just saying they are going to make changes will not suffice. Journaling can be therapeutic as well as a way to begin identifying goals for greater intellectual well-being.

4. GOAL-SETTING
Step 4 will remind participants not to give up and to be persistent in their efforts to develop greater intellectual capacities. Explain that this takes time and that they should not expect immediate results. The purpose of setting goals is to help each participant take smaller steps leading to the selected overall goal. Encourage participants to review and revise their plans to develop thinking and learning skills that lead to success and happiness. By developing MBM goals to work toward and achieve, participants will remain motivated while they slowly learn how to live well intellectually.

5. MONITORING MY BEHAVIOR
Step 5 will help participants to see the progress they are making in developing intellectual functioning. This will assist participants to be accountable, persistent, and motivated to enhance mental and intellectual competence. You should act as coach and encourage participants to develop and utilize their newfound intellectual skills.

6. REWARD YOURSELF
Step 6 will ensure that participants reward themselves as they achieve their intellectual goals. Remind participants to reward themselves as they improve. Healthy and meaningful rewards provide them with positive feedback and motivation to continue creating their own intellectual well-being.

7. TIPS
Step 7 will allow participants to grow from reading and implementing the various tips, which are included as suggestions for processing each session.

Motivational Barriers to Behavioral Change

With intellectual wellness comes the ability to think clearly, pick up on new ideas, be open-minded and accepting of others creative and imaginative styles, and embrace learning new things. However, changing behavior is not an easy task; there are many barriers to successful behavioral change. Participants must remain motivated for their behaviors to change exist. When participants begin to see their behavior changing, they will feel more confident and enthusiastic in approaching new learning situations. Therefore, as the facilitator, you need to be aware of any barriers that may be keeping participants from being successful as they work to live happier, intellectually well lives.

Motivation is one of the keys to success in reaching personal and professional goals. Motivation is an inner desire to reach a goal through effective action. Following are some of the keys in overcoming motivational barriers:

- Motivation can be accomplished through negative and positive means. Negative motivation is usually accomplished through the use of punishment. This is probably not the preferred method to use when trying to motivate oneself. Instead, one should rely on positive motivation or rewards to ensure that positive intellectual well-being continues.

- Some people feel very motivated when they begin to learn new skills. Think about how many times you have you set New Year's resolutions. When you do, you probably feel very motivated when you begin, but you fall back into less effective old habits. The secret to making long-lasting behavioral changes is to work toward your goals at a steady pace.

- Failure, like success, is just a result of taking action. One of the biggest motivational barriers is fear of failure, or fear that the outcome will turn bad. Accept that one will not ALWAYS be successful in efforts to make major behavioral changes. One may not make all of the desired changes, but that doesn't mean one must stop what one is doing. Encourage participants to give their best and hope for the best.

- One may get bored if one works on changing the same intellectual weakness for too long. Boredom can kill motivation. Encourage participants to try to work on several aspects of their intellectual well-being whenever they feel they're on the verge of burning out and giving up.

Enhanced intellectual well-being has been shown to contribute to one's ability to cope with stressors and enhance creativity, self-esteem, and longevity. In working to enhance mental functioning, one needs to remember that thoughts can influence emotions and behaviors. Therefore, it is important to understand one's thoughts and mental functioning to be more intellectually well. Emotions have the quality of alerting people that something is wrong in their lives and something needs to be changed. This workbook is designed to help your participants function more effectively, embrace lifelong learning, and be open to new ideas.

Using this Workbook to Modify Behavior

Behavior Modification programs provide a process to PERMANENTLY change destructive and inefficient ways of thinking and replace them with positive ones that will lead to greater health and well-being. The behavior modification program included in this series of workbooks contains several critical steps:

Motivated Behavior Modification (MBM) Components

STEP 1: Self-Assessment – The first step in modifying behavior involves determining the frequency, circumstances, and outcomes of the mental functions to be altered or enhanced. MBM relies on objective self-assessment to determine the participants' intellectual functioning to establish a baseline for their strengths and limitations. Once a baseline is established, the data collected can be used to track participants' progress through the mental functions that are being addressed. The self-assessments contained in this workbook are referred to as "formative assessments" and can be used to assess participants' current level of functioning and also to measure intellectual functioning change over time.

In this stage, people acknowledge that they have a problem and begin to seriously think about making healthier lifestyle changes. They want to explore in depth the level of their difficulties in changing ineffective mental functioning. Self-assessments are very powerful tools for helping participants learn more about themselves to gain valuable insights into their constructive and destructive ways of thinking, to better understand themselves, and to gain valuable insights into their thinking, feelings and behaviors. Self-assessments allow facilitators to gather information about participants to get a complete picture of each person.

Facts about self-assessments:

- Self-assessments provide you with a small sample of behavior and should not be used to stereotype participants. Self-assessments are designed to allow participants to explore their behavioral strengths and weaknesses.
- Factors such as cultural background, handicaps, and age should be taken into consideration when exploring self-assessment results.
- Self-assessments are designed to be self-administered, scored and interpreted by the participants. However, facilitators should be available to assist participants in understanding their scores in an objective and helpful way.
- Self-assessments are designed to gather self-reported data, thus the results are dependent on each participant's motivation and cooperation.
- Self-assessment results should be explored in light of other behavioral data that facilitators have available, not in isolation.
- Self-assessments can be used with individual participants or with groups.
- Self-assessments can be used to form specific decisions about the type of instruction that would be most beneficial. Thus, if your group scores lowest on a particular self-assessment in a section, that might be an effective place to concentrate instruction.
- Participants can use the results of their self-assessments to adjust and improve their behavior.

(Continued on the next page)

Using this Workbook to Modify Behavior

Motivated Behavior Modification (MBM) Components *(Continued)*

STEP 2: Support System – The next step in behavior modification involves participants recognizing who is in their support system and specifically identifying which people are supportive of which topics. This requires participants to think about who can support them through each particular behavior modification, what their supporters can do, and how their supporters will help. Support people may vary for each behavior. The person who is being supportive about mental sharpness can be different from the one being supportive about exploring lifelong learning.

STEP 3: Journaling – The next step in behavior modification is journaling answers to specific questions. Journaling has been shown to be very effective in helping people to think critically about themselves and issues they are coping with. It is wise to remind participants not to concern themselves with grammar or spelling. Just free-writing thoughts and ideas is the purpose of the journal.

STEP 4: Goal Setting – The next step in behavior modification is to set goals to modify behavior. Goals initiate an action plan, and motivate and guide behavioral change. Participants will set goals that will replace their old, negative habits with new, healthier and positive habits. It is important to help participants determine which specific behaviors they want to change. This will help to give order and context to the change process. Goals provide participants with direction, priorities and a well-conceived action plan for MBM. Goals should meet these criteria:

- **Specific and Behavioral:** Goals must be stated in concrete, behavioral terms. For example, *"I would like to begin studying at the community college"* would be a concrete, behavioral goal.
- **Measurable:** Goals must be measurable so that people can track their progress. For example, *"I want to learn something"* is too vague to be measured accurately, but *"I want to study Spanish at the community college starting in the fall semester"* can be measured.
- **Attainable:** Goals must be within reach or participants will not be motivated to work toward them. They must feel that they have a realistic opportunity to achieve their goals. For example,*"I will apply for admissions to the community college by May"* is an attainable goal.
- **Relevant:** Goals must be important to the participant. For example, learning a second language can help keep a person's brain young, and aid in communicating with people in the community will help to provide motivation.
- **Time-Specific:** Goals must have specific times for completion if they are going to have power. However, the time frames need to be reasonable and realistic so that participants will feel comfortable with their commitment. For example, by setting a goal of *"I want to apply for admissions to the community college by summer so I can begin taking classes in the fall"* sets a realistic time frame to accomplish the goal.

The goal setting process helps participants to be personally accountable in changing their unhealthy behaviors.

STEP 5: Monitoring – The next step is to monitor behaviors until desired outcomes are reached. Sections will be included for participants to keep a regular record of their activities and progress. Motivation is the intrinsic drive that pushes participants into action and makes permanent behavioral changes. Motivation is enhanced when participants are working toward specific goals and monitoring their progress as they continue to make motivated behavioral modifications. By monitoring their progress as they move toward goals, participants reinforce MBM.

STEP 6: Rewards – This step defines rewards for accomplishing behavioral goals. Healthy and meaningful rewards will vary from person to person. Participants will benefit by rewarding themselves for any positive steps taken to change unhealthy behaviors.

STEP 7: Tips – This final step provides insights into ways people can deal with unwanted behaviors.

Introduction for the Participant

Many people focus on emotional wellness in their overall wellness plans. However, in recent years, intellectual wellness has come to the forefront as a critical component in the overall wellness and life satisfaction of people. Your mind has a striking influence on your emotional wellness and your physical wellness. In fact, research indicates that your thinking actually triggers many of your emotional reactions, and your thinking also can lead to physical ailments.

Intellectual wellness is critical to your overall well-being. People who are intellectually well, tend to be independent thinkers, open to new ideas, interested in lifelong learning, curious and creative, and able to pick up on new ideas and concepts. In addition, they are able to concentrate, focus, and remember people, places and events.

People enjoy many benefits from maintaining emotional wellness:

- You will be more interested in learning in and outside of the classroom.
- You will be more creative.
- You will learn the connection between thoughts and feelings.
- You will be better able to use common sense.
- You will be more open-minded and accepting of others and their ideas.
- You will more trusting of your own ideas and not need to rely solely on the ideas of "experts."
- You will be able to approach learning situations with eagerness.
- You will be able to think critically.
- You will develop effective and efficient thinking skills.
- You will see how your mind can open up new avenues of exploration.

As you can see, you have many reasons to develop intellectual wellness skills and habits. The biggest challenge is to find ways to learn about your mental functioning so that you can develop the mindset to be a creative, critical and independent thinker.

The purpose of the *Intellectual Well-Being Workbook* is to help you understand the relationship between mental functioning and your overall well-being, and to keep you motivated while you modify your thought-related behaviors. In this workbook, you will engage in various types of self-assessments. You will have an opportunity to set effective intellectual goals and look forward to living a healthier life.

(Continued on the next page)

Introduction for the Participant *(Continued)*

Some Things to Remember

Developing effective intellectual behaviors can be difficult, as is implied in the adage "It's difficult to teach an old dog new tricks!" Developing your mental functions can be a challenging task, but by completing the activities in this workbook, your goals can be accomplished.
You can do this!

- Take one step at a time. By working on one behavior at a time, the task of changing your behavior will not feel insurmountable. Because mental functions are so difficult to develop, it is important to start with small mental functions and work slowly to change one at a time. By trying to change more than one behavior at a time, people set themselves up for failure. Keep it simple!

- Create a support system to help you develop your intellectual functioning. Who can you ask for help and support in modifying your intellectual functions? Choose people with whom you feel comfortable, people who would be helpful in a specific area of your life, and people who know that you are trying to make changes. You don't have to suffer in silence to successfully develop new, more effective thinking skills. Let people know about your desire to change and allow others to support you.

- Write everything down on paper. Saying you are going to make changes will not suffice. Self-assessments, working on defined behaviors and writing concrete goals that you set for yourself will help you to be successful.

- Be persistent in your efforts and do not give up on yourself. Remember that it takes time to change ingrained thinking patterns. Do not expect immediate results. The purpose of setting goals is to help you take smaller steps leading to your overall goal. Plan for a healthier lifestyle. By developing Motivated Behavior Modification (MBM) goals to work toward and achieve, you will remain motivated while you slowly turn unhealthy or lazy habits into healthy and ambitious ones.

- Be accountable. If during your efforts to make positive changes you slip and go back to old thinking habits, don't let this stop you. Attempt to learn from your setbacks and use your newfound knowledge to make successful choices to move forward. Monitor your progress.

- Reward yourself for a job well done. HEALTHY and meaningful rewards provide you with positive feedback and motivate you to continue in your efforts to develop greater intellectual well-being. You will find ways to reward yourself for each job well done.

- Use the tips, as applicable to you, provided on the last page of each of the sessions.

You are now prepared to begin making Motivated Behavior Modifications (MBMs)! Working through the steps in each section of this workbook will allow you to more easily change ineffective thinking to effective thinking. This process really works. It is an exciting way to change your thinking patterns so that you can begin to enjoy and appreciate a happier, healthier life.

Table of Contents

Section I – Open to New Ideas

Section II – Lifelong Learning

Section III –Thinking Skills

Table of Contents

Table of Contents

Section VII – Independent Thinking

SECTION I

OPEN TO NEW IDEAS

There is much to be gained
from opening the door to your mind
and letting new ideas and beliefs
come in.

– Senora Roy

Name ______________________________

Date ______________________________

OPEN TO NEW IDEAS

Step 1: Self-Assessment Introduction and Directions

Intellectually well people are open to new ideas. They are open to different ways of thinking about the complexities of the world and issues confronted by society. This type of thinking is often referred to as divergent thinking. Being open to new ideas is vital to making effective decisions, exhibiting personal creativity and innovativeness, and understanding yourself better.

The purpose of the *Open to New Ideas Self-Assessment* is to help you explore how open you are to new and different ideas in your personal and professional life. This self-assessment contains three individual scales. Read each statement carefully and circle the number of the response that describes you best.

Do not pay attention to the numbers, just the headings:

- Usually True
- Rarely True
- Not True

In the following example, the circled 3 indicates the statement is usually true of the person completing the scale:

	USUALLY TRUE	RARELY TRUE	NOT TRUE
1. I come up with unique solutions to problems	(3)	2	1

This is not a test and there are no right or wrong answers. Do not spend too much time thinking about your answers. Your initial response will be the most true for you. Be sure to respond to every statement.

Turn the page and complete the Self-Assessment

OPEN TO NEW IDEAS

Step 1: Self-Assessment Scales

	USUALLY TRUE	RARELY TRUE	NOT TRUE
1. I come up with unique solutions to problems	3	2	1
2. I can generate wild ideas that often work	3	2	1
3. I rarely look at things in new ways	1	2	3
4. I am not good at solving unusual problems	1	2	3
5. I am innovative in solving problems	3	2	1
6. I conceptualize problems differently from other people	3	2	1
7. I enjoy repetitive tasks	1	2	3
8. I don't enjoy the problem solving process	1	2	3
9. I am good at brainstorming creative ideas	3	2	1
10. I like to approach problems in new ways	3	2	1

I. TOTAL = _________

11. I am open-minded to change	3	2	1
12. I am not able to adapt easily	1	2	3
13. I have lots of new ideas	3	2	1
14. I am not spontaneous	1	2	3
15. I have strong views and will not sway away from them	1	2	3
16. I like to learn about new topics	3	2	1
17. I have trouble taking positive, calculated risks	1	2	3
18. I like ideas that challenge my beliefs	3	2	1
19. I will not change what I think	1	2	3
20. I cannot change how I view the world	1	2	3

II. TOTAL = _________

21. I can form images in my mind	3	2	1
22. I fantasize a lot	3	2	1
23. I like to think of new possibilities	3	2	1
24. I don't have many memories from the past	1	2	3
25. I picture images in my mind	3	2	1
26. I have a vivid imagination.	3	2	1
27. I can build mental scenes in my mind that do not exist	3	2	1
28. I have difficulty thinking of possibilities for myself	1	2	3
29. I often imagine tastes or smells from my past	3	2	1
30. I have trouble picturing the outcomes of two alternatives in my mind	1	2	3

III. TOTAL = _________

Go to the Scoring Directions on the next page

OPEN TO NEW IDEAS

Step 1: Self-Assessment Scoring Directions

People find themselves in situations where they run out of ideas. The self-assessment you just completed is designed to help you explore how open you are to develop, and to use thinking, that is outside of the traditional box. On the previous page, total the circles in each scale and write them on the line marked TOTAL. Then transfer that number below. Next, add your three scores to get your *Open to New Ideas Self-Assessment* total score.

I. Outside the Box Scale Total = ________

II. Ideas Scale Total = ________

III. Imagination Scale Total = ________

Open to New Ideas Self-Assessment Total Score = ________

Profile Interpretation

Find the range for your scores and use the information below to assist you in the interpretation of your scores.

Total Individual Scale Scores	Total Self-Assessment Score	Result	Indications
Scores from 24 to 30	Scores from 71 to 90	High	You are very open to the ideas of others, are able to think outside the box, and have an imagination that allows you to discover novel solutions to problems.
Scores from 17 to 23	Scores from 51 to 70	Moderate	You are somewhat open to the ideas of others, are somewhat able to think outside the box, and have an imagination that sometimes allows you to discover novel solutions to problems.
Scores from 10 to 16	Scores from 30 to 50	Low	You are not very open to the ideas of others, have difficulty thinking outside the box, and have a limited imagination that holds you back from discovering novel solutions to problems.

Regardless of your score on the individual scales or the total self-assessment, all of the exercises that follow have been designed to help you develop openness to new ideas.

Go to the Scale Descriptions on the next page

OPEN TO NEW IDEAS

Step 1: Scale Descriptions

Outside the Box – This scale is designed to measure your ability to think from a new and different perspective. People scoring high on this scale are usually able to think in novel ways. They are able to move past obvious ways of operating to generate unconventional ideas.

Ideas – This scale is designed to measure how you generate ideas. People scoring high on this scale will listen and evaluate new perspectives, explore the value of non-traditional ideas, and strive to create new and improved ways of getting things done.

Imagination – This scale is designed to measure your imagination. People scoring high on this scale are able to see mental images in their mind of things that exist, as well as the ability to imagine objects, situations or circumstances that do not exist now. They are able to visualize mental images, sounds, tastes, smells or sensations.

Step 2: Recognize and Develop a Support System

Supportive people in your life can help you to develop your intellectual wellness. People in your support system can encourage and help you to explore possibilities to develop your imagination, think outside the box and be open to new ideas.

Complete the following table with people who might be in your support system.

Supporter	How This Person Can Support Me	How I Can Contact This Person
My friend Kathy	*She likes hearing about my ideas.*	*Email: Kathy@ooo.com*

Keep this list handy. Call, email or text when you need support.

OPEN TO NEW IDEAS

Step 3: Keep a Journal – My Openness

The following journal questions are designed to help you explore how open your mind is to new ideas. Remember, your thinking can affect how motivated you are to make healthy changes in your behavior.

Write about a time you thought outside the box.

Write about a time you creatively solved a problem.

Write about how you generate new ideas. Alone? Brainstorming with others? Taking a Walk? Tell how this works for you.

Write about a time you used your imagination to solve a problem.

Write about a way you can be open to new ideas.

OPEN TO NEW IDEAS

Step 4: Set Goals

Having an open mind leads to living a full life. Being flexible and able to think in new ways is important when you encounter new experiences and ideas. For your action plan, identify the behavior you want to change and the specific goals required for you to take, in order to reach your ultimate goal; the behavior that will help you to be more receptive and open to new ideas, which is necessary for your intellectual well-being.

The behavior I want to change ________________________________

Goals need to be SMART:

Specific, **M**easureable, **A**ttainable, **R**ealistic and **T**ime-Specific

Goals	How I Will Measure This Goal	How This Goal Is Attainable and Realistic?	Time Deadline	How This Will Help Me
Have less arguments with members of my blended family	*Less amount of verbal confrontations*	*I can be more flexible and open-minded with ALL family members.*	*6 months*	*I will have less stress and more family harmony.*

If you are having trouble identifying goals, consult TIPS, page 30.

OPEN TO NEW IDEAS

Step 5: Monitor My Behavior – Outside the Box

Monitoring your progress toward your openness to new ideas will help ensure that you are becoming more imaginative and able to think outside of the box. Keeping track of your behaviors through logs will help you determine what you have accomplished at given times. Periodic re-evaluations support your success. Once you reach your goal(s), set new ones to improve or maintain what you have already achieved. Use a separate page for each innovative behavior you want to develop.

EXAMPLE:

My "outside of the box" behavior change *Form a different perspective when trying to solve problems*

My goal *Learn to brainstorm ideas with trusted friends*

Date	My Accomplishment	How It Felt
1/1/2014	*I brainstormed some ideas with Joe*	*I feel like there are some possibilities*

Outside the Box

My "outside of the box" healthy behavior change ________________

My goal ________________

Date	My Accomplishment	How It Felt

(Continued on the next page)

OPEN TO NEW IDEAS

Step 5: Monitor My Behavior

Outside the Box *(Continued)*

For what problem are you having a difficult time finding a solution? ______________________

____

____

With whom does this problem occur? ______________________________________

____

Is this problem at work, in school, in the home, in the community, or somewhere else? __________

____

____

How do you typically solve your problems, or find solutions to your problems? ______________

____

____

Who can help you solve this problem? ______________________________________

Is there any reason not to ask this person for help? ______________________________

____

Think outside of the box. What are a few possibilities of actions you can take to solve this problem?

____

____

____

____

____

____

(Continued)

OPEN TO NEW IDEAS

Step 5: Monitor My Behavior – Ideas

Openness to ideas and different ways of thinking about the world and the issues that emerge from our complex society is important in decision-making, problem solving and creativity. Keeping track of your behaviors through logs will help you determine what you have accomplished at given times. Periodic re-evaluations support your success. Once you reach your goal(s), set new ones to improve your ability to generate ideas for life's every day solutions. Use a separate page for each change.

EXAMPLE:

My "new idea" behavior change *Change how I think about people from cultures other than mine*

My goal *Learn more about other cultures*

Date	My Accomplishment	How It Felt
1/1/2014	*I traveled to another country*	*I was shocked at the stereotypes I held that were just not true!*

Ideas

My "new idea" behavior change ______________________________

My goal ______________________________

Date	My Accomplishment	How It Felt

(Continued on the next page)

OPEN TO NEW IDEAS

Step 5: Monitor My Behavior – Ideas *(Continued)*

Do you consider yourself flexible or rigid? Explain. ______

______

______

Do you consider yourself open to new ideas or closed? Explain. ______

______

______

What was a time you were presented with a new idea, refused it and were so glad? ______

______

______

What was a time you were presented with a new idea, refused it and were sorry later? ______

______

______

What was a time you were presented with a new idea, immediately open to it, and sorry later? ______

______

______

What was a time you were presented with a new idea, immediately open to it, and it worked out great.

______

______

How does this quotation from Edward de Bono relate to you?

Studies have shown that 90% of error in thinking is due to error in perception. If you can change your perception, you can change your emotion and this can lead to new ideas.

______

______

______

OPEN TO NEW IDEAS

Step 5: Monitor My Behavior – Imagination

Having an active imagination can help you be intellectually healthy! Monitoring your progress toward your goals will help to reinforce your openness to new ideas. Keeping track of your behaviors through logs will help you determine what you have accomplished. Periodic re-evaluations support your success. As you achieve your use of imagination goals, set new ones to improve or maintain what you have already achieved. Use a separate page for each way you want to develop your imagination.

EXAMPLE:

My "imaginative" behavior change *To begin imagining more possibilities for myself in my career*

My goal *To imagine my "perfect" career in the future, and then develop ideas of how to achieve this image*

Date	My Accomplishment	How It Felt
1/1/2014	*I began reading about successful business people*	*Empowered*

Imagination

My "imaginative" behavior change____

My goal ____

Date	My Accomplishment	How It Felt

(Continued on the next page)

OPEN TO NEW IDEAS

Step 5: Monitor My Behavior – Imagination *(Continued)*

How would you describe your imagination? ____________________________

In what ways do you use your imagination? ____________________________

What is an example of a time when you used your imagination and it enhanced your intellectual growth?

How does your imagination help in solving problems? ____________________________

How do you use your imagination by picturing images in your mind? ____________________________

What has been a barrier to your using your imagination? ____________________________

OPEN TO NEW IDEAS

Step 6: Reward Myself

Hopefully, you are becoming aware of why it is important to be open to new ideas, and also to learn how to begin enhancing your current functioning in these areas! Congratulations! You need to give yourself a pat on the back or some other meaningful reward. People who reward themselves are more likely to remain open to new ideas than people who don't! Your reward needs to be something that will give you the incentive to continue to think outside the box. It needs to be healthy, within your budget and something you'll be excited about. If you are buying yourself something, be sure your reward is something you wouldn't ordinarily buy or do. Brainstorm some possible rewards.

- Rewards that would be meaningful to me ____________________
- Small rewards I could give myself ____________________
- Large rewards I could give myself ____________________
- Things that would not cost money and would be fun ____________________
- Rewards that I can afford and that would be fun ____________________
- Rewards that I enjoy alone ____________________
- Rewards I enjoy with people who support me ____________________

You deserve a pat on the back for the hard work you are completing in this section. Rewards help you to pay attention to your triumphs, not your setbacks. Rewards will create good feelings and propel you to want to work harder to reach your goals. Whenever you have completed or achieved one of your goals, treat yourself to one of the items on your list.

You can also reward yourself by giving yourself positive affirmations when you have achieved a goal. Below are some samples. Cut them out and post them in visible spots at home and work! If these don't work for your goal, write your own on sticky notes!

I am creative and resourceful.	A different perspective is a good thing!	Being creative is a joy.
I can think outside the box!	*I can be an innovator!*	I let my imagination soar!
I am imaginative.	**I am an idea machine!**	*I am open-minded!*

Albert Einstein said, *"Imagination is everything. It is the preview of life's coming attractions."*

What does this quote mean to you? ____________________

____

OPEN TO NEW IDEAS

Step 7: Tips For Motivated Behavior Modification

Outside the Box

- Try to look at a situation or task from a different perspective.
- Think differently with an open mind and find new ways of functioning creatively.
- Challenge your assumptions and beliefs. Where did they come from? Just because some things have always been done a certain way does not mean that they must continue to be done that way.
- Break pre-conceived norms or rules to get ideas or the solutions you need. Try doing something backwards to get a new perspective.
- Gather a few people together and free-style, brainstorm solutions.

Ideas

- When you have ideas, jot them down to avoid forgetting them.
- Brainstorm for ideas. When brainstorming, state ideas regardless of how different they sound at the time. Write down all ideas and then revisit them at a later time.
- Get away from habits and routines. When you do, you will find that the mental habits which are stifling your creativity will disappear.
- As you daydream, jot down ideas that simply pop into your head. Because your subconscious continues to work while daydreaming, you will generate more creative ideas than when you are concentrating on a task.
- Keep a piece of paper and pencil by your bedside. If, during the night, a thought pops into your head, write it down and go back to sleep. There might be more!

Imagination

- Be creative and try different ways of thinking by engaging in puzzles like crossword puzzles, number puzzles, jigsaw puzzles, etc.
- Read books that will take you to new worlds. This will allow you to experience sights and sounds that do not exist in your present world. Regardless of the plot of the book, think about new ways that the story could have ended.
- Think about stores, businesses, and online shops where you interact and how you could improve upon their products, packaging, logo, service, etc. Think about ways (in your mind) that you could envision each working more effectively.
- Try new hobbies and activities such as learning a new language or researching a new country you know nothing about. You will look at the activity from a different perspective.
- Try a guided imagery CD to help you visualize.

SECTION II

LIFELONG LEARNING

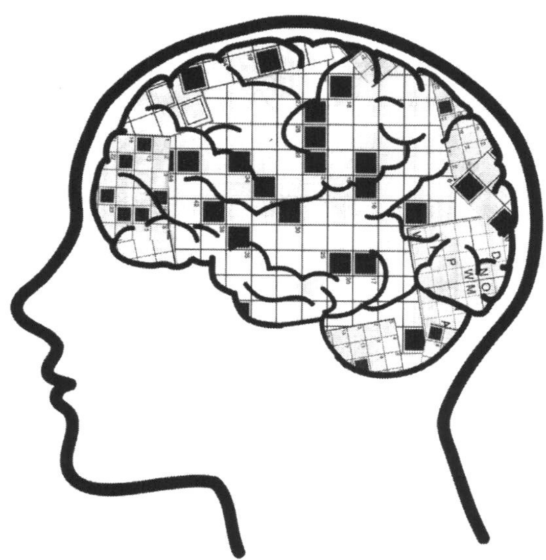

Anyone who stops learning is old,
whether at twenty or eighty.
Anyone who keeps learning stays young.

– Henry Ford

Name ______________________________

Date ______________________________

LIFELONG LEARNING

Step 1: Self-Assessment Introduction and Directions

People who embrace the concept of lifelong learning tend to be more intellectually healthy. Lifelong learning has many health and wellness benefits, and people who practice lifelong learning, regardless of their age, will see improved mental and physical health, relationships, life-styles and careers. People who are lifelong learners believe that on-going learning will improve their lives and improve their overall intellectual wellness.

The *Lifelong Learning Self-Assessment* is designed to help you identify how much of a lifelong learner you are. This self-assessment contains three individual scales. Read each statement carefully and circle the number of the response that describes you best.

In the following example, the circled 1 indicates the statement is not at all descriptive of the person completing the scale:

3 = LIKE ME **2 = A LITTLE LIKE ME** **1 = NOT LIKE ME**

When it comes to learning ...

I like to upgrade my general knowledge base. 3 2 (1)

This is not a test. Since there are no right or wrong answers, do not spend too much time thinking about your answers. Be sure to respond to every statement.

Turn the page and complete the Self-Assessment

LIFELONG LEARNING

Step 1: Self-Assessment Scales

3 = LIKE ME **2 = A LITTLE LIKE ME** **1 = NOT LIKE ME**

When it comes to learning ...

I like to upgrade my general knowledge base	3	2	1
I am interested in new technologies	3	2	1
I look for opportunities to learn anything new	3	2	1
I believe education is more than the process of going to school	3	2	1
I am interested in learning how to think	3	2	1
I enjoy learning things outside of a traditional classroom	3	2	1
I continually search for activities to stimulate my mind	3	2	1

M. TOTAL = ________

When it comes to learning ...

I participate in intellectual discussions	3	2	1
I keeping abreast of current affairs in my community	3	2	1
I read about national and international affairs	3	2	1
I attend plays, lectures, musicals, and performances	3	2	1
I enjoy creative and artistic activities	3	2	1
I like stimulating mental games and activities	3	2	1
I like to engage in intellectually stimulating projects	3	2	1

I. TOTAL = ________

I believe that learning ...

Greatly improves my life and my career	3	2	1
Enhances my self-concept	3	2	1
Gives me the tools to learn how to think	3	2	1
Increases my appreciation for the arts	3	2	1
Keeps my mind young	3	2	1
Will increase my income	3	2	1
Will help me benefit my community	3	2	1

B. TOTAL = ________

Go to the Scoring Directions on the next page

LIFELONG LEARNING

Step 1: Self-Assessment Scoring Directions

Lifelong learning consists of three critical aspects: motivation, interests and benefits. The self-assessment you just completed is designed to help you explore how much you believe in, and take part in, lifelong learning. On the previous page, total the circles in each scale and write them on the line marked TOTAL. Then transfer that number below. Next, add your three scores to get your *Lifelong Learning Self-Assessment* total score.

M. Motivation Scale Total = ________

I. Interests Scale Total = ________

B. Benefits Scale Total = ________

Lifelong Learning Self-Assessment Total Score = ________

Profile Interpretation

Find the range for your scores and use the information below to assist you in the interpretation of your scores.

Total Individual Scales Scores	Total Self-Assessment Score	Result	Indications
17 to 21	50 to 63	High	If you scored between 17 and 21 on any scale, you embrace the value of lifelong learning. The activities will help you to continue valuing lifelong learning.
12 to 16	35 to 49	Moderate	If you scored between 12 and 16, you somewhat embrace the value of lifelong learning. The activities will help you continue to see the value of lifelong learning.
7 to 11	21 to 34	Low	If your score was between 7 and 11, you rarely embrace the value of lifelong learning. The activities will help you see the value of lifelong learning.

Regardless of your score on the individual scales or the total self-assessment, all of the exercises that follow have been designed to help you with lifelong learning.

Go to the Scale Descriptions on the next page

EMBRACE LIFELONG LEARNING

Step 1: Scale Descriptions

Motivation – People scoring high on this scale are motivated to continue learning throughout their lives. They are interested in learning new things and keeping up with new technologies. They believe that learning continues long after formal education stops.

Interests – People scoring high on this scale have a variety of interests. They are interested in continuing to learn through intellectual conversations, mentally-stimulating games, reading and research, and creative activities.

Benefits – People scoring high on this scale understand the many benefits of continuing their learning. They understand that learning keeps their mind young and they recognize the value of education in their lives, careers, and how they view themselves.

Step 2: Recognize and Develop a Support System

In order to be more of a lifelong learner, you need people who will support you and be available to you when you need them. Not every person in your life will be helpful for each of your challenges. Complete the following table with people who might be able to support you in expressing your emotions effectively.

Supporter	How This Person Can Support Me	How I Can Contact This Person
My Friend Nellie	*Go to a seminar or class with me.*	*Phone only: 123-4567*

Keep this list handy. Call, email or text when you need support.

LIFELONG LEARNING

Step 3: Keep a Journal

Reflecting on and journaling about how important education is in your life can be therapeutic. Following are some journaling exercises that can help you think about the behaviors related to the motivation, interest and benefits of ongoing education. Remember, your intellectual wellness is directly related to your participation in lifelong learning.

What would you like to learn more about? Where can you get this additional education? ____________

What new technologies would you like to learn? ____________

What learning activities would help to stimulate your brain? ____________

What artistic and creative activities do you enjoy? Which ones would you like to try? ____________

What type of learning will allow you to earn more money? ____________

What can you learn more about to feel good about yourself? ____________

(Continued on the next page)

LIFELONG LEARNING

Step 3: Keep a Journal of My Learning *(Continued)*

It is important to keep track of the learning opportunities in your life. Using this page, identify all of the learning options (inside and outside the classroom) that you either currently enjoy or might like, how you can engage in them or begin engaging in them, and how they help you.

Learning Opportunities I Enjoy

A Learning Opportunity I Enjoy	How Often I Engage in This	How This Learning Opportunity Helps Me

Learning Opportunities I Might Enjoy

A Learning Opportunity I MIGHT Enjoy	How Much Time I Can Devote to This	How This Learning Opportunity Can Help Me

LIFELONG LEARNING

Step 4: Set Goals

A well-conceived action plan will help to motivate you as you begin and/or continue with more lifelong learning activities. Identify the behavior you want to change, and the specific goals required for you to take, in order to reach your ultimate goal; the behavior that will help you engage in lifelong learning.

The behavior I want to change ______________________________

Goals need to be SMART:

Specific, **M**easureable, **A**ttainable, **R**ealistic and **T**ime-Specific

Goals	How I Will Measure This Goal	How This Goal Is Attainable and Realistic?	Time Deadline	How This Will Help Me
To be active in the local book club in my community	*The number of times I go to club meetings*	*I think I have time to read a book each month*	*2½ weeks*	*I will read about different things and meet new people in the book club*

If you are having trouble identifying goals, consult TIPS, page 45.

LIFELONG LEARNING

Step 5: Monitor My Behavior – Motivation

People who embrace lifelong learning are motivated to engage in learning activities inside and outside of the classroom. They want to enhance their knowledge base and be mentally stimulated. Periodic re-evaluations support your efforts to continue engaging in your current (and new) learning experiences. Once you reach your goal(s), set new ones to improve or maintain what you have already achieved. Use a separate page for each change.

EXAMPLE:

My "motivational" behavior change *Learn latest technologies for communicating*

My goal *To be able to communicate with my grandchildren more easily*

Date	My Accomplishment	How It Felt
1/1/2014	*I bought a better cell phone*	*I was excited to talk more easily with them*

Motivation

My "motivational" behavior change ____________________

My goal ____________________

Date	My Accomplishment	How It Felt

(Continued on the next page)

EMBRACE LIFELONG LEARNING

Step 5: Monitor My Behavior – Interests

Intellectually well people are interested in learning through a variety of venues. Monitoring your interest in learning can help to enhance your mental functioning. Keeping track of your intellectual interest will help you determine what you have accomplished and what you need to continue working on. Periodic re-evaluations support your success, improve or maintain what you have already achieved and motivate you. Use a separate page for each change.

EXAMPLE:

My "interest in learning" behavior change *Train my brain better*

My goal *Do a crossword puzzle each day to keep my brain young*

Date	My Accomplishment	How It Felt
1/1/2014	*I started doing the daily crossword puzzle*	*It was fun and I felt like I was using my mind*

Interest

My "interest in learning" behavior change ____________________

My goal ____________________

Date	My Accomplishment	How It Felt

(Continued on the next page)

EMBRACE LIFELONG LEARNING

Step 5: Monitor My Behavior – Benefits

Engagement in intellectual activities brings many different types of benefits such as feeling better about yourself, earning more money, becoming more interesting to be with, and keeping your brain young. Use the following chart to monitor your progress toward your goals, re-inforce your behavior, and determine what you have accomplished at given times. Periodic re-evaluations will help you create new learning goals. Once you reach your goal(s), set new ones to improve or maintain what you have already achieved. Use a separate page for each change.

EXAMPLE:

My "benefits" behavior change *To find a better job by learning new technologies*

My goal *Learn how to develop websites*

Date	My Accomplishment	How It Felt
1/1/2014	*I registered for a class in web design at the community college*	*I feel excited about new career opportunities*

Benefits

My "benefits" behavior change ____________________

My goal ____________________

Date	My Accomplishment	How It Felt

(Continued on the next page)

JOURNAL PROCESSING

Step 5: Lifelong Learning *(Continued)*

MOTIVATION

What new technologies would you like to learn more about? How will you do it?

How will you upgrade your knowledge base?

INTERESTS

What mentally-stimulating games do you enjoy? How do these games help you stay mentally sharp?

What creative/artistic activities do you enjoy watching? Which do you enjoy engaging in?

BENEFITS

How can lifelong learning enhance your professional life? How can it improve your personal life?

How does lifelong learning help to keep your brain young?

EMBRACE LIFELONG LEARNING

Step 6: Reward Myself

When you engage in a new, or continue, in current learning experiences, you need to reward yourself! For most people, it can be awkward to reward yourself. Regardless, you will find that you are more likely to repeat behaviors if you do find a way to give yourself a reward. Your reward should give you the incentive to achieve your goals, be within your budget and be something you'll be excited about. If you are buying yourself something, be sure your reward is something you wouldn't ordinarily buy or do. **Brainstorm some possible rewards.**

- Rewards that would be meaningful to me ____________________
- Small rewards I could give myself ____________________
- Large rewards I could give myself ____________________
- Things that would not cost money and would be fun ____________________
- Rewards that I can afford and that would be fun ____________________
- Rewards that I enjoy alone ____________________
- Rewards I enjoy with people who support me ____________________

You deserve a pat on the back for the hard work you are completing in this section. Rewards help you to pay attention to your triumphs, not your setbacks. Rewards will create good feelings and propel you to want to work harder to reach your goals.

Whenever you have completed or achieved one of your goals, treat yourself to one of the items on your list. You can also reward yourself by giving yourself positive affirmations when you have achieved a goal. Below are some samples. Cut them out and post them in visible spots at home and work! If these don't work for your goal, write your own on sticky notes!

I am a quick study.	*Learning keeps me young!*	I can learn anything I want to.
I am smarter every day!	*I will keep learning!*	I apply what I learn to what I am doing!
I'm never too old to stop learning.	**Learning stimulates my brain.**	*I am curious and like to learn.*

"The excitement of learning separates youth from old age. As long as you're learning you're not old."

~ Rosalyn S. Yalow

EMBRACE LIFELONG LEARNING

Step 7: Tips For Motivated Behavior Modifications

MOTIVATION

- Keep a learning to-do list. As you think of new things you would like to learn, write them down and then go back and explore ways you can actually learn about them.
- Teach others. The best way to learn something new is to do the research to teach it to others.
- Read and collect posts from blogs of interest. This can be the impetus to begin engaging in a new learning experience.
- Keep a Learning Journal to become more aware of new things you might be interested in learning more about.
- Forced learning is an interesting way to learn new things. If you have never liked math, you might try doing Sudoku.

INTERESTS

- Explore learning opportunities in your community. Identify programs at local community colleges and YMCA/YWCA centers.
- Start your own learning group based on a subject in which you have an interest. For example, if you are interested in learning more about other cultures, you might start a group that shares pictures and stories from travel adventures.
- Join an organization that teaches new skills. For example, your local animal shelter probably teaches new ways of training and caring for pets.
- Hang around people who have learning interests similar to yours.
- Try a new cultural experience, one you've never tried before: new museum, concert, theater, zoo, opera, etc.

BENEFITS

- Lifelong learning allows you to develop more of an open mind. Use this type of learning to examine other sides of issues of interest.
- The more learners discover about history, current events, politics, or the culture of other countries, the more they want to learn.
- Lifelong learning can help you explore (and discover) meaning in your life.
- Lifelong learning helps us make new friends and establish valuable relationships.
- People who keep learning are better able to maintain their memory and they age gracefully.

SECTION III

THINKING SKILLS

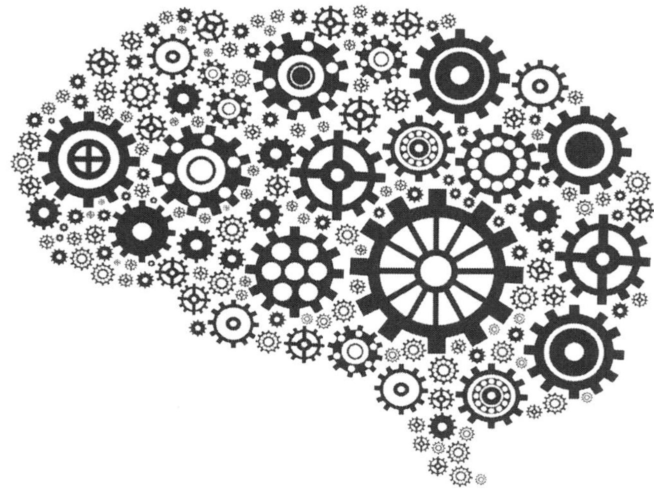

Never be afraid to sit awhile and think!

– Lorraine Hansberry, A Raisin in the Sun

Name ______________________________

Date ______________________________

THINKING SKILLS

Step 1: Self-Assessment Introduction and Directions

People use a variety of thinking skills in their interactions with other people and their environment. Whether you believe it or not, your thinking patterns play an important role in determining how you make decisions and behave. Therefore, they are critical in how well you live your life.

The *Thinking Skills Self-Assessment* is designed to build your awareness of the effectiveness of your thinking skills in everyday life. Read each statement carefully and circle the number of the response that describe you best.

Do not pay attention to the numbers, just the headings:

- Usually like me
- Not usually like me
- Not like me

In the following example, the circled 3 indicates the statement is not like the person completing the self-assessment:

	USUALLY LIKE ME	NOT USUALLY LIKE ME	NOT LIKE ME
1. I don't handle transitions easily	1	2	(3)

This is not a test and there are no right or wrong answers. Do not spend too much time thinking about your answers. Your initial response will be the most true for you. Be sure to respond to every statement.

Turn the page and complete the Self-Assessment

THINKING SKILLS

Step 1: Self-Assessment Scales

	USUALLY LIKE ME	NOT USUALLY LIKE ME	NOT LIKE ME
1. I don't handle transitions easily	1	2	3
2. I multi-task and move from one task to another easily	3	2	1
3. I am able to maintain my focus for extended periods of time	3	2	1
4. I do not think before reacting or responding to others	1	2	3
5. I work in a logical manner	3	2	1
6. I can maintain sustained attention despite noises	3	2	1
7. I am unable to reflect on several ideas at one time	1	2	3
8. I consider a wide range of solutions when I have a problem	3	2	1

P - TOTAL = ________

	USUALLY LIKE ME	NOT USUALLY LIKE ME	NOT LIKE ME
9. I have trouble thinking hypothetically	1	2	3
10. I can envision possibilities for the problems in life.	3	2	1
11. I get in trouble when my life becomes unpredictable.	1	2	3
12. I do not handle vagueness well	1	2	3
13. I don't mind new and novel situations and experiences.	3	2	1
14. I try to understand both sides of a disagreement.	3	2	1
15. I tend to be a black and white thinker	1	2	3
16. I can handle deviations from my original plans	3	2	1

F - TOTAL = ________

	USUALLY LIKE ME	NOT USUALLY LIKE ME	NOT LIKE ME
17. I do not think rationally	1	2	3
18. I become emotional when I am frustrated or angry	1	2	3
19. I can manage my thoughts when I am irritable	3	2	1
20. I can change my thinking to become less anxious	3	2	1
21. I can reverse my negative thoughts to positive ones	3	2	1
22. I pay attention to my internal self-talk	3	2	1
23. I do not express emotional thoughts	1	2	3
24. I view situations in a positive way	3	2	1

E - TOTAL = ________

Go to the Scoring Directions on the next page

THINKING SKILLS

Step 1: Self-Assessment Scoring Directions

Intellectually healthy people are able to control and use their thinking powers to help them navigate life situations more effectively. The self-assessment you just completed is designed to help you explore your thinking skills. On the previous page, total the circles in each scale and write them on the line marked TOTAL. Then transfer that number below. Then add your three scores to get your *Thinking Skills Self-Assessment* total score.

P. Processing Scale Total = ________

F. Flexibility Scale Total = ________

E. Emotional Regulation Scale Total = ________

***Thinking Skills Self-Assessment* Total Score** = ________

Profile Interpretation

Total Individual Scale Scores	Total Self-Assessment Score	Result	Indications
Scores from 19 to 24	Scores from 56 to 72	High	You use many thinking skills that handle everyday situations with efficiency and effectiveness.
Scores from 14 to 18	Scores from 40 to 55	Moderate	You have some thinking skills that allow you to handle everyday situations with efficiency and effectiveness.
Scores from 8 to 13	Scores from 24 to 39	Low	You need to develop your thinking skills that will allow you to handle everyday situations with efficiency and effectiveness.

Regardless of your score on the individual scales or the total self-assessment, all of the exercises that follow have been designed to help you develop additional thinking skills.

Go to the Scale Descriptions on the next page

THINKING SKILLS

Step 1: Scale Descriptions

Processing – People who score high on this scale tend to be able to handle transitions well and find solutions to everyday problems. They are logical and able to maintain focus and attention on tasks, but also move smoothly from task to task if necessary.

Flexibility – People who score high on this scale tend to be able to think flexibly and handle uncertainty and vagueness in life. They are not upset in new and novel situations and are able to handle the unpredictability of life.

Emotional Regulation – People who score high on this scale tend to think rationally and understand how their thinking corresponds with their feelings and behavior. They are able to monitor their negative thinking and change it to more positive thinking.

Step 2: Recognize and Develop a Support System

Recognizing your strengths and weaknesses in thinking can greatly enhance your life satisfaction. To do so, you need the support of people you know who can help. Not every supportive person in your life will be helpful with this, but some will. Complete the following table with people who might be able to support you in your efforts to develop more effective thinking skills.

Supporter	How This Person Can Support Me	How I Can Contact This Person
My co-worker TJ	*When there is a change at work, he goes with the flow. He can help me do that.*	*Phone or text: 000-0001, email: james22@.com*

Keep this list handy. Call, email or text when you need support.

THINKING SKILLS

Step 3: Keeping a Journal
Thinking = Behavior and Emotions

Journaling is an excellent way for you to truly look at your behaviors and emotions resulting from your thinking. The questions that follow have been designed to help you think with an open mind about your current behaviors. Remember, your thinking can affect how you manage the change and stress in your life.

What are some of the big changes in your life?__________

How and when does your thinking affect how you handle these changes? __________

How and when does your thinking positively affect your emotions or behavior?__________

How does your thinking negatively affect your emotions or behavior? __________

When you get angry or frustrated, what are you thinking about?__________

What keeps you from moving easily from one task to another? __________

How does your inner self-talk impact your thinking and behaving? __________

How does uncertainty and vagueness affect your thinking? __________

THINKING SKILLS

Step 4: Set Goals

Action planning is an important step in achieving lasting behavioral changes. Action planning will ensure you remain motivated in your efforts to learn and practice effective thinking skills. For your action plan, identify both the specific behaviors you want to change, and develop goals and smaller steps required to reach your intellectual wellness goals.

The behavior I want to change ______________________________

Goals need to be SMART:

Specific, **M**easureable, **A**ttainable, **R**ealistic and **T**ime-Specific

Goals	How I Will Measure This Goal	How This Goal Is Attainable and Realistic?	Time Deadline	How This Will Help Me
To think at least one positive thought each day	*Keep track of the number of times I have positive thoughts each week*	*I can change my thinking one day at a time*	*One week*	*I will be more enjoyable to be around*

If you are having trouble identifying goals, consult TIPS, page 60.

THINKING SKILLS

Step 5: Monitor My Behavior – Processing

Life is full of transitions that require you to move from task to task easily. It is very helpful to have the ability to maintain focus and find solutions to everyday problems. The chart below will help you keep track of your goals. Identify some goals and then periodically re-evaluate them. Once you reach your goal(s), set new ones to improve or maintain what you have already achieved. Use a separate page for each change.

EXAMPLE:

My "processing" behavior change *To solve daily problems rationally and carefully*

My goal *To learn more creative solutions to solve problems*

Date	My Accomplishment	How It Felt
1/1/2014	*I tried a brainstorming technique*	*I developed a wider range of options and it felt great*

Processing

My "processing" behavior change ______________________________

My goal ______________________________

Date	My Accomplishment	How It Felt

(Continued on the next page)

THINKING SKILLS

Step 5: Monitor My Behavior – Flexibility

Life is unpredictable and processing information related to this unpredictability is important. It helps to be able to be flexible in your thinking process and handle uncertainty and vagueness in your life. The chart below will help you keep track of your work life goals. Identify some work life goals and then periodically re-evaluate them. Once you reach your work life goal(s), set new ones to improve or maintain what you have already achieved. Use a separate page for each change.

EXAMPLE:

My "flexibility" behavior change *To be able to handle the uncertainty of possible layoffs in a calm way*

My goal *To stop worrying about my job security*

Date	My Accomplishment	How It Felt
1/1/2014	*I started doing the daily crossword puzzle*	*It was fun and I felt like I was using my mind*

Flexibility

My "flexibility" behavior change ______________________________

My goal ______________________________

Date	My Accomplishment	How It Felt

(Continued on the next page)

THINKING SKILLS

Step 5: Monitor My Behavior – Emotional Regulation

Your thinking affects your feelings and your behavior. Being able to monitor and understand the effects of negative thinking (and changing this thinking to more positive thinking) is a critical skill necessary in everyday life. Think about, write down, and then monitor your goals for your personal life. Don't forget to periodically re-evaluate. Once you reach your personal life goal(s), set new ones to improve or maintain what you have already achieved. Use a separate page for each change.

EXAMPLE:

My "emotional regulation" behavior change *Connect my negative thinking to my moods*

My goal *Recognize my negative thinking and change it*

Date	My Accomplishment	How It Felt
1/1/2014	*I actually realized how negative I became when I was angry, and adjusted my thoughts*	*Satisfying*

Emotional Regulation

My "emotional regulation" behavior change____________________

My goal____________________

Date	My Accomplishment	How It Felt

(Continued on the next page)

JOURNAL PROCESSING

Step 5: Thinking Skills *(Continued)*

PROCESSING

How do you react when facing multiple problems at one time? How could you react more effectively?

What transitions have you handled well? Which ones have you not handled well and why?

FLEXIBILITY

What types of uncertainties make you nervous? How can you deal with uncertainty more easily?

How do you deal with new situations? How can you be more flexible in dealing with unpredictability?

EMOTIONAL REGULATION

When do you get extremely emotional? How can you better control your emotions with rational thinking?

In what situations do you find yourself thinking negatively? How can you change negative thoughts to more positive thinking?

THINKING SKILLS

Step 6: Reward Myself

When you engage in a new, or continue, in current learning experiences, you need to reward yourself! For most people, it can be awkward to reward yourself. Regardless, you will find that you are more likely to repeat behaviors if you do find a way to give yourself a reward.

Your reward should give you the incentive to achieve your goals, be within your budget and be something you'll be excited about. If you are buying yourself something, be sure your reward is something you wouldn't ordinarily buy or do. Remember that some of the best things in life are free.

Brainstorm some possible rewards.

- Rewards that would be meaningful to me ____________________
- Small rewards I could give myself ____________________
- Large rewards I could give myself ____________________
- Things that would not cost money and would be fun ____________________
- Rewards that I can afford and that would be fun ____________________
- Rewards that I enjoy alone ____________________
- Rewards I enjoy with people who support me ____________________

You deserve a pat on the back for the hard work you are completing in this section. Rewards help you to pay attention to your triumphs, not your setbacks. Rewards will create good feelings and propel you to want to work harder to reach your goals. Whenever you have completed or achieved one of your goals, treat yourself to one of the items on your list.

You can also reward yourself by giving yourself positive affirmations when you have achieved a goal. Below are some samples. Cut them out and post them in visible spots at home and work! If these don't work for your goal, write your own on sticky notes!

My thinking skills can and will improve in quality.	***I am flexible!***	I can be spontaneous.
I can find solutions to my problems!	*I can work hard to become a positive thinker!*	I am okay with unpredictability.
I ask good questions to help me learn.	**I interpret information correctly.**	*I can manage my thoughts and my feelings.*

Buddha urged us, *"What we think, we become!"* How do you do that? ____________________

____

____

THINKING SKILLS

Step 7: Tips For Motivated Behavior Modification

Processing

- Think outside the box when you encounter problems that need solving.
- Decide which is more successful for you – multi-tasking or tunnel vision. Then, do it.
- Focus on a problem and then let go and think about something completely different. This will trigger the right side of your brain and prompt "Aha!" creativity.
- Try meditating to enhance your ability to focus.
- Find ways to avoid distractions.

Flexibility

- Ask yourself, "Am I being flexible or inflexible in this situation?"
- Embrace new experiences.
- Be aware of when and where you're being inflexible. Is it in your thinking? Is it your way of doing things at home or at work, or is it with someone in particular?
- When you are stuck in inflexibility your emotions may be clouding your inner thinking. You might have expectations of how things "should be" and be quick to jump to assumptions, conclusions, and falsities stemming from the ego's need to be right, or in control.
- Consider taking healthy risks.

Emotional Regulation

- Keep a thought log of how your thinking is impacting your feelings and behavior.
- Confront your negative thinking by recognizing its faulty premise.
- Therefore, if you think "I can't do anything right!" you can recognize that this is an overgeneralization and that you have been able to do many things right.
- Be aware of when your thinking includes thinking such as "you should…" or "you ought…"
- Remember that if you are constantly experiencing anxiety, depression or anger, you are engaging in excessive amounts of negative thoughts. Remember that it is not the situation that is causing your feeling, but the way you are thinking about that situation.
- Monitor your automatic negative thoughts.

SECTION IV

CREATIVE THINKING

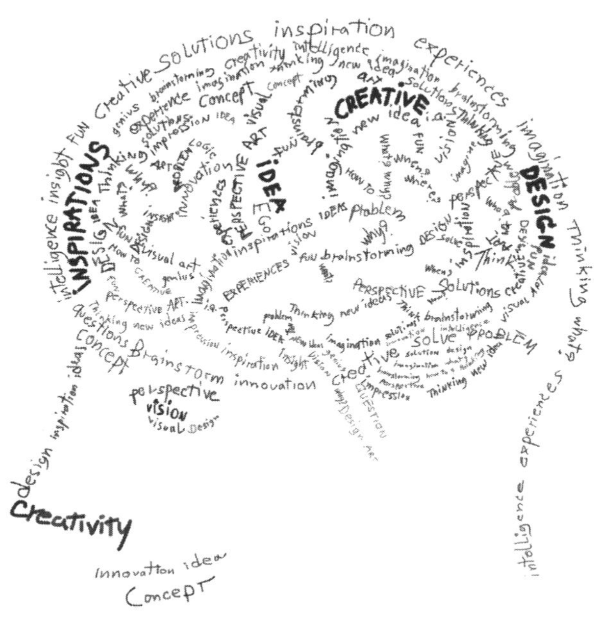

You see things and ask "Why?"
I dream things that never were
and ask "Why not?"

– George Bernard Shaw

Name ____

Date ______________________________

CREATIVE THINKING

Step 1: Self-Assessment Introduction and Directions

Most people are creative in one way or another. When you think of creativity, visions of writers, musicians, singers, and artists probably come to the forefront of your mind. In reality there are many different forms of creativity including creating things, solving problems, developing ideas, exploring a new approach or creating new technology systems.

The purpose of the *Creative Thinking Self-Assessment* is to help you explore how well you are able to visualize, experience and express your creativity. This self-assessment contains three individual scales. Read each of the statements carefully and decide whether or not the statement describes you. If the statement does describe you, circle the YES next to that item. If the statement does not describe you, circle the NO next to that item.

Do not pay attention to the numbers, just the headings:

- Yes
- No

In the following example, the circled number under "Yes" indicates the statement is descriptive of the person completing the scale.

	YES	NO
I have a distinct vision of what is possible	(2)	1

This is not a test. Since there are no right or wrong answers, do not spend too much time thinking about your answers. Be sure to respond to every statement.

Turn the page and complete the Self-Assessment

CREATIVE THINKING

Step 1: Self-Assessment Scales

	YES	NO
I have a distinct vision of what is possible	2	1
I am able to see far-fetched possibilities	2	1
I am able to see the *bigger picture*	2	1
I am afraid to try anything new	1	2
I am able to see only what already exists	1	2
I have flashes of creative insight	2	1
I discover new ideas in my sleep	2	1
I have *off-the-wall* ideas that often work out	2	1

A. TOTAL = ______

	YES	NO
I am an intuitive thinker	2	1
I make time to use my imagination	2	1
I tend not to be very curious	1	2
I am curious and look for better ways to do things	2	1
I am playful and spontaneous	2	1
I don't believe that creativity is that important	1	2
I have trouble accepting uncertainty	1	2
I am critical of new or different ideas from others	1	2

B. TOTAL = ______

	YES	NO
I have had little exposure to creative experiences	1	2
I express my personality in creative ways	2	1
I rarely immerse myself in creative activities	1	2
I find enjoyment in being creative	2	1
I express my creativity ideas even if I don't get great reactions	2	1
I involve others in my creative process	2	1
I have fun with activities and ideas	2	1
I have many passions and/or creative interests	2	1

C. TOTAL = ______

Go to the Scoring Directions on the next page

CREATIVE THINKING

Step 1: Self-Assessment Scoring Directions

Creative people think in new ways and respond to change with new and innovative ideas. They are able to combine ideas and information in ways that allow for completely new ideas, products, solutions and processes. On the previous page, total the circles in each scale and write them on the line marked TOTAL. Then transfer that number below. Then add your three scores to get your *Creative Thinking Self-Assessment* total score.

A. Visualizing Scale Total = ________

B. Experiencing Scale Total = ________

C. Expressing Regulation Scale Total = ________

***Creative Thinking Self-Assessment* Total Score** = ________

Profile Interpretation

Total Individual Scales Scores	Total Self-Assessment Score	Result	Indications
Scores from 14 to 16	Scores from 41 to 48	High	You have many of the characteristics of people who are able to express their creativity.
Scores from 11 to 13	Scores from 32 to 40	Moderate	You have some of the characteristics of people who are able to express their creativity.
Scores from 8 to 10	Scores from 24 to 31	Low	You need to develop characteristics of people who are able to express their creativity.

Regardless of your score on the individual scales or the total self-assessment, all of the exercises that follow have been designed to help you develop openness to new ideas.

Go to the Scale Descriptions on the next page

CREATIVE THINKING

Step 1: Scale Descriptions

Visualizing – People scoring high on this scale are able to see possibilities, visualize mental pictures of what may be possible, and have innovative ideas. They have creative intuitions and are not afraid to try and implement their creative ideas.

Experiencing – People scoring high on this scale are intuitive and imaginative. They have a great deal of curiosity and are always looking for better ways to do things. They enjoy playing with new ideas and are spontaneous and flexible in their approach.

Expressing – People scoring high on this scale have experienced a variety of creative activities and enjoyed them. They enjoy expressing their unique personality characteristics through their creative activities and thoroughly enjoy spending their time being creative.

Step 2: Recognize and Develop a Support System

Engaging in creative activities is challenging. It helps to have creative people to talk with and to collaborate with. Complete the following table with people who might be able to support you in developing and maintaining a creative outlook in life.

Supporter	How This Person Can Support Me	How I Can Contact This Person
My Father	*By continually reminding me to search (like he does) for new ways of doing things.*	*phone 000-000-0000*

Keep this list handy. Call, email or text when you need support.

CREATIVE THINKING

Step 3: Keep a Journal – Ways I Am, or Could Be, Creative

Journaling can definitely help you in exploring how creative you are in life, and also identify the barriers keeping you from being more creative. These journaling items will help you to explore how well you have integrated creativity into your everyday life. Please complete the following items so that you can better understand your creative instincts.

In what ways are you creative? ______________________________

____

____

What types of creative risks are you willing to take? ______________________________

____

____

How does your creativity help you come up with ideas to solve problems? ______________________________

____

____

What keeps you from being as creative as you might be? ______________________________

____

____

How can you overcome those obstacles? ______________________________

____

____

Who or what zaps your energy? ______________________________

____

____

How can you be creative and do something about that situation? ______________________________

____

____

CREATIVE THINKING

Step 4: Set Goals

It will help your creative juices to flow if you are able to adjust to change and life problems comfortably. To do so, you need to develop creativity goals. These are goals that you can work toward, and when completed, will motivate you to do more! For your action plan below, identify ways that you can be more creative in life and your career.

The behavior I want to change ____

Goals need to be SMART:
Specific, **M**easureable, **A**ttainable, **R**ealistic and **T**ime-Specific

Goals	How I Will Measure Each Goal	How Each Goal Is Attainable and Realistic	Time Deadline	How This Change Will Help Me
I want to start painting again	*If I can find a certain designated time each week*	*I can give up a few hours of TV on the weekend*	*One month*	*I will feel so accomplished*

If you are having trouble identifying goals, consult TIPS, page 74.

CREATIVE THINKING

Step 5: Monitor My Behavior – Visualizing

Being able to see the big picture and possibilities in situations is a key to the creative process. Setting creativity-related goals and monitoring your progress toward those goals will help to reinforce your ability to develop creative ideas and visualize possibilities in your mind. The chart below will guide you through the development and tracking of creativity goals. Review your behaviors periodically to ensure you are progressing in your pursuit of enhanced creativity. Once you reach a goal, set new ones to continue to develop creativity in your life. Use a separate page for each change.

EXAMPLE:

My "visualizing" behavior change *I will mentally picture different ways to complete tasks*

My goal *I will make at least one disliked task more enjoyable each week*

Date	My Accomplishment	How It Felt
1/1/2014	*I made a very difficult dessert recipe and served it for dinner first!*	*It was fun to do because I pictured everyone's surprise!*

Visualizing

My "visualizing" behavior change ______________________

My goal ______________________

Date	My Accomplishment	How It Felt

(Continued on the next page)

CREATIVE THINKING

Step 5: Monitor My Behavior – Experiencing

If you are not a curious person, you are not alone. Many people live their lives without exploring areas outside of their comfort zones. Use the chart below to set some goals to work toward being more curious and willing to take risks. Monitor your behavior to help you determine how successful you have been in developing a sense of curiosity. Once you reach your goal(s), set new ones to improve or maintain what you have already achieved. Use a separate page for each change.

EXAMPLE:

My "experiencing" behavior change *I will express curiousity by asking appropriate questions*

My goal *To learn something new about each person in my life*

Date	My Accomplishment	How It Felt
1/1/2014	*I was able to be more engaged by asking interesting and appropriate questions*	*I felt like a more interested and interesting person*

Experiencing

My "experiencing" behavior change ______________________________

My goal ______________________________

Date	My Accomplishment	How It Felt

(Continued on the next page)

CREATIVE THINKING

Step 5: Monitor My Behavior – Expressing

A creative attitude and outlook is possible for all people to enjoy. However, you will need to begin and continue engaging in creative activities. In the spaces that follow, identify some of the goals you have for enhancing your creativity. These goals should be related to seeing opportunities, taking risks, and expressing yourself in creative pursuits of interest. Monitoring your progress toward these types of goals will help you develop a creative attitude. Keep track of your behaviors through the table below, re-evaluate your success, and then set new goals to enhance what you have already achieved. Use a separate page for each change.

EXAMPLE:

My "expressing" behavior change *I will find a creative way to express who I am*

My goal *To begin enjoying a creative interest that matches my personality*

Date	My Accomplishment	How It Felt
1/1/2014	*I made arrangements to take guitar lessons*	*I think I will be able to express myself through music*

Expressing

My "expressing" behavior change ______________________________

My goal ______________________________

Date	My Accomplishment	How It Felt

(Continued on the next page)

JOURNAL PROCESSING

Step 5: Creative Thinking *(Continued)*

VISUALIZING

What innovative ideas have you had in the past? What do you have for the future?

What possibilities do you foresee for your future? How can you make them happen?

EXPERIENCING

In what ways are you intuitive? How do you receive intuitive ideas?

What are you curious about? What do you want to learn more about?

EXPRESSING

In what ways are you creative? How do you express this creativity?

If you do not immerse yourself in creative activities, why not?

(Continued on the next page)

CREATIVE THINKING

Step 6: Reward Myself

Creativity is a skill that anyone can acquire. There are specific ways to enhance your creativity, and you have learned many of them in this section. As you complete goals and find yourself becoming more creative, you need to reward yourself. Your reward needs to be something that will give you the incentive to achieve even more goals. It needs to be within your budget and something you'll be excited about. If you are buying yourself something, be sure your reward is something you wouldn't ordinarily buy or do. **Brainstorm some possible rewards.**

- Rewards that would be meaningful to me ____________________
- Small rewards I could give myself ____________________
- Large rewards I could give myself ____________________
- Things that would not cost money and would be fun ____________________
- Rewards that I can afford and that would be fun ____________________
- Rewards that I enjoy alone ____________________
- Rewards I enjoy with people who support me ____________________

You deserve a pat on the back for the hard work you are completing in this section. Rewards help you to pay attention to your triumphs, not your setbacks. Rewards will create good feelings and propel you to want to work harder to reach your goals. Whenever you have completed or achieved one of your goals, treat yourself to one of the items on your list.

You can also reward yourself by giving yourself positive affirmations when you have achieved a goal. Below are some samples. Cut them out and post them in visible spots at home and work! If these don't work for your goal, write your own on sticky notes!

I have an inquisitive mind.	***I can find solutions to my problems.***	*I see opportunities everywhere.*
I will let my imagination soar!	*I am a naturally curious person.*	I will take calculated risks.
I can allow my curiosity to growby asking questions.	**Creativity exists in me!**	*Creativity is joyful and fun!*

"Dance above the surface of the world. Let your thoughts lift you into creativity that is not hampered by opinion."

~ Red Haircrow

CREATIVE THINKING

Step 7: Tips For Motivated Behavior Modification

VISUALIZING

- By visualizing a wide perspective, you may discover causes and effects, as well as hidden solutions.
- Allow yourself to see mental pictures in your mind.
- Use affirmations such as "I can do things creatively in my life."
- Keep a list of all of the creative activities that come into your mind. Once you have developed your list, start working on it.
- Don't allow people or things to drain your energy.

EXPERIENCING

- Establish a place where you can go for your creative work. This place could be in a part of your house, a café, a neighbor's house, or simply a desk in the corner of a room.
- Follow your passions.
- Pay attention to the inner and outer signals that lead to a creative experience. Inner messages can come from intuition, dreams, daydreams and coincidences. Outer messages come from your environment in the form of sights, sounds, and conversations.
- Spend time alone to experience curiosity and imagination in solitude.
- Open yourself to the creative process. Allow yourself to be playful and spontaneous with others.

EXPRESSING

- Prepare for, but do not give in or over-react, to any criticism you receive from others.
- Find the form of creative expression that suits you best.
- Take time out to explore various forms of expression. Envision yourself engaging in a variety of different types of creative activities.
- Go to museums, science exhibits, galleries, concerts, theater, the zoo, etc. Observe what *sings out* to you.
- Spend time in your local library. Read books about writing, movies, entrepreneurs, dancers, musicians, etc.

SECTION V

CRITICAL THINKING

If you think you can, you can.
And if you think you can't, you're right.

– Mary Kay Ash

Name ____

Date ______________________________

CRITICAL THINKING

Step 1: Self-Assessment Introduction and Directions

Critical thinking is your ability to question what you read and hear, create new ideas, use information to solve problems and make decisions, and look at life from a long-term, big-picture perspective.

The purpose of the *Critical Thinking Self-Assessment* is to help you explore how well you are able to visualize, experience and express your creativity. This self-assessment contains three individual scales. Read each of the statements carefully and decide whether or not the statement describes you. If the statement does describe you, circle the YES next to that item. If the statement does not describe you, circle the NO next to that item.

Do not pay attention to the numbers, just the headings:

- Yes
- No

In the following example, the circled number under "Yes" indicates the statement is descriptive of the person completing the scales.

	YES	NO
I always want to know the truth	(2)	1

This is not a test and there are no right or wrong answers. Do not spend too much time thinking about your answers. Your initial response will be the most true for you. Be sure to respond to every statement.

Turn the page and complete the Self-Assessment

CRITICAL THINKING

Step 1: Self-Assessment Scales

	YES	NO
I always want to know the truth	2	1
I trust what authorities tell me	1	2
I am hungry for facts and concepts	2	1
I accept everything I see and read	1	2
I rarely question what others tell me	1	2
I enjoy exploring new ideas	2	1
I am able to apply the insight I gain from information I find	2	1

I - TOTAL ______

	YES	NO
I am not open to changes	1	2
I can easily see others' points of view	2	1
I respect the rights of others to express different opinions	2	1
I believe problems have only one good solution	1	2
I look forward to hearing the opinions of others	2	1
I listen to others with an open mind	2	1
I am curious and like to learn more	2	1

II - TOTAL ____

	YES	NO
I know when ideas require supporting evidence	2	1
I cannot easily break down complicated information	1	2
I easily analyze problems and come up with solutions	2	1
I see a situation from various viewpoints	2	1
I have trouble analyzing information	1	2
I evaluate the validity of what I read and hear	2	1
I can distinguish relevant from irrelevant facts	2	1

III - TOTAL ____

Go to the Scoring Directions on the next page

CRITICAL THINKING

Step 1: Self-Assessment Scoring Directions

Critical thinking is self-guided, self-disciplined thinking which seeks to reason at the highest level of quality in a fair-minded way. People who think critically consistently attempt to live their lives thinking rationally, reasonably and emphatically. The *Critical Thinking Self-Assessment* is designed to help you explore how careful and astute you are in believing or not believing all of the information from others, including the media. On the previous page, total the circles in each scale and write them on the line marked TOTAL. Then transfer that number below. Then add your three scores to get your *Critical Thinking Self-Assessment* total score.

I. Seek the Truth Scale Total = ________

II. Be Open Minded Scale Total = ________

III. Think Analytically Scale Total = ________

***Critical Thinking Self-Assessment* Total Score** = ________

Find the range for your scores and use the information below to assist you in the interpretation of your scores.

Profile Interpretation

Total Individual Scale Scores	Total Self-Assessment Score	Result	Indications
Scores from 12 to 14	Scores from 35 to 42	High	You have many of the qualities of people who exhibit critical thinking in their lives. The activities that follow will help you build even stronger critical thinking skills.
Scores from 10 to 11	Scores from 29 to 34	Moderate	You have some of the qualities of people who exhibit critical thinking in their lives. The activities that follow will help you build even stronger critical thinking skills.
Scores from 7 to 9	Scores from 21 to 28	Low	You have a few of the qualities of people who exhibit critical thinking in their lives. The activities that follow will help you build even stronger critical thinking skills.

No matter how you scored on the Scale (Low, Moderate or High), you will benefit from all of the following exercises.

Go to the Scale Descriptions on the next page

CRITICAL THINKING

Step 1: Scale Descriptions

Seek The Truth – People scoring high on this scale want to know the truth in life, they seek facts about their subjects, and do not blindly accept everything they read and hear. They do not trust everything from people who seem to know, they question others and seek their own conclusions.

Be Open Minded – People scoring high on this scale are open to possibilities. They are able to easily see and understand the viewpoint of others, even if they don't agree, and are even anxious to hear these opinions. They have an open-minded curiosity.

Think Analytically – People scoring high on this scale are analytical thinkers. They analyze most things that people say and do, as well as information they receive, for accuracy. They look at their own problems through multiple points of view, and can easily break down and think about complex information.

Step 2: Recognize and Develop a Support System

There are times when people are unable to analyze situations and think as critically as they would like. When this happens they can use a support system; people who are able to remind them of your need to seek the truth, remain open-minded and analyze information critically. Complete the following table with people who might help you to feel good about yourself.

Supporter	How This Person Can Support Me	How I Can Contact This Person
My Significant Other	*He often reminds me of when I am being taken in by a biased newscaster.*	*At home, call or text*

Keep this list handy. Call, email or text when you need support.

CRITICAL THINKING

Step 3: Keep a Journal – Seeking the Truth

Critical thinking can help you achieve your personal and professional goals more easily and accurately. The following questions are designed to help you think conscientiously about how you think and what you want to change. Share your honest thoughts and emotions.

Why would you, or other people, want to seek the truth?______________________

____

____

What or whom do you tend to readily accept when you see, hear or read it? ______________

____

____

What do you find yourself questioning the most? ______________________

____

____

Whom do you find yourself questioning the least? ______________________

____

____

How would you describe your open-mindedness about others thoughts and opinions?__________

____

____

How would you describe your closed-mindedness about others thoughts and opinions?__________

____

____

How can you become a more effective critical thinker?______________________

____

____

CRITICAL THINKING

Step 4: Set Goals

Critical thinking is a skill that people need in order to be more intellectually alert. Critical thinkers are able to analyze information before accepting it and then accept the opinions of others only with significant documentation. For your action plan, identify the critical thinking issues you want to change, set specific goals to achieve this change, and notice how much better you are able to make decisions and solve problems.

The behavior I want to change ______________________________

Goals need to be SMART:

Specific, **M**easureable, **A**ttainable, **R**ealistic and **T**ime-Specific

Goals	How I Will Measure Each Goal	How Each Goal Is Attainable and Realistic	Time Deadline	How This Change Will Help Me
I will not join the bandwagon when co-workers gossip. I will form my own opinions.	*I will make note of each time I am able to ignore or challenge their comments.*	*Concentrate on positive things people say*	*One month*	*I will have fewer doubts about others, which will help me to be more positive about work.*

If you are having trouble identifying goals, consult TIPS, page 88.

CRITICAL THINKING

Step 5: Monitor My Behavior – Seek the Truth

Critical thinkers are interested in seeking and finding the truth about information they receive. They seek out facts and ideas that can verify information. One way is to begin to set goals for becoming more of a truth seeker. In the chart that follows, set some goals to begin questioning what authorities are telling you, what you are reading on the Internet, or what you are watching on TV. Periodic re-evaluation of your goals will help you become more critical more quickly. Once you reach a goal, set new ones to improve or maintain what you already feel. Use a separate page for each change.

EXAMPLE:

My "truth seeking" behavior change *Begin questioning what others say about which foods are healthy*

My goal *Learn a better system for critically examining information*

Date	My Accomplishment	How It Felt
1/1/2014	*I used valid websites on the Internet to search for accurate knowledge*	*It felt great!*

Seek the Truth

My "truth seeking" behavior change ______________________

My goal ______________________

Date	My Accomplishment	How It Felt

(Continued on the next page)

CRITICAL THINKING

Step 5: Monitor My Behavior – Open-Minded

Open-minded people are better able to listen to and adopt the viewpoints of others, if these views are realistic and accurate. Set some goals to enhance your open-mindedness. The following guide is designed to do just that. By setting goals and working toward them, you will develop critical thinking skills. Keep reviewing these goals and setting new ones to work toward. Use a separate page for each change. Notice how much better your thinking is!

EXAMPLE:

My "open-minded" behavior change *To ask about opinions that differ from mine*

My goal *To weigh the pros and cons of different perspectives*

Date	My Accomplishment	How It Felt
1/1/2014	*I listened to the opinions of my brother, with whom I always disagree*	*It felt good as I tried to put myself in his shoes. I still didn't agree but understood where he was coming from*

Open-Minded

My "open-minded" behavior change ______________________________

My goal ____

Date	My Accomplishment	How It Felt

(Continued on the next page)

CRITICAL THINKING

Step 5: Monitor My Behavior – Think Analytically

Analytical thinkers require supporting evidence before they blindly accept the opinions and judgments of others. Try to think more, identify some goals that you can work toward. Monitor your progress and keep track of your results below. Occasionally re-evaluate your results and develop new goals to improve your critical thinking abilities. Use a separate page for each change.

EXAMPLE:

My "analytical thinking" behavior change *Examine and evaluate the statements of others*

My goal *Evaluate the validity of the things my neighbor tells me*

Date	My Accomplishment	How It Felt
1/1/2014	*I will search for evidence to support or dispute facts in our conversations*	*I felt better about my neighbor when I realized he was only guessing and there was no truth in his statements*

Think Analytically

My "analytical thinking" behavior change ____________________

My goal ____________________

Date	My Accomplishment	How It Felt

(Continued on the next page)

JOURNAL PROCESSING

Step 5: Critical Thinking – Evaluation *(Continued)*

SEEK THE TRUTH

What types of information do you blindly accept? ______________________

____

What types of information do you research? ______________________

____

Whose opinions do you trust? ______________________

____

Whose opinions do you not trust? ______________________

____

BE OPEN-MINDED

To what types of possibilities are you open? ______________________

____

To what types of possibilities are you not open? ______________________

____

Whose viewpoints do you value? ______________________

____

Whose viewpoints do you not value? ______________________

____

THINK ANALYTICALLY

In what aspects of your life do you think analytically? ______________________

____

In which aspects do you not think analytically? ______________________

____

What process can you use to examine ideas through multiple viewpoints? ______________________

____

CRITICAL THINKING

Step 6: Reward Myself

When you think critically about information, it is easier to attain intellectual well-being. It is interesting that when you begin to think critically, you begin to feel better about yourself. To do so, you will need to reward yourself when you behave in a way that makes you feel good about yourself. People who reward themselves are more likely to work to achieve the same emotions again! The challenge is to decide what reward would motivate you to reach your goals. Your reward needs to be something that will give you the incentive to achieve your goals. It needs to be within your budget and something you'll be excited about. If you are buying yourself something, be sure your reward is something you wouldn't ordinarily buy or do. **Brainstorm some possible rewards.**

- Rewards that would be meaningful to me ____________________
- Small rewards I could give myself ____________________
- Large rewards I could give myself ____________________
- Things that would not cost money and would be fun ____________________
- Rewards that I can afford and that would be fun ____________________
- Rewards that I enjoy alone ____________________
- Rewards I enjoy with people who support me ____________________

You deserve a pat on the back for the hard work you are completing in this section. Rewards help you to pay attention to your triumphs, not your setbacks. Rewards will create good feelings and propel you to want to work harder to reach your goals. Whenever you have completed or achieved one of your goals, treat yourself to one of the items on your list.

You can also reward yourself by giving yourself positive affirmations when you have achieved a goal. Below are some samples. Cut them out and post them in visible spots at home and work! If these don't work for your goal, write your own on sticky notes!

I am an analytical thinker.	***I will examine that idea.***	I form my own unbiased opinions.
I live a truthful life and have the right to expect truth from others.	*I continually process information.*	I seek the truth.
I am a critical thinker.	**I come to sensible solutions.**	*I do not accept the words of others unconditionally.*

"If there was one life skill everyone on the planet needed, it was the ability to think with critical objectivity."

– Josh Lanyon

THINK CRITICALLY

Step 7: Tips For Motivated Behavior Modification

Seek The Truth

- Distinguish facts from opinions. Facts are information based on objective reality, while opinions are a belief or judgment, not necessarily based in objective reality.
- Decide how important TRUTH is to you - to yourself, to others, and from others.
- Challenge your assumptions and the assumptions of other people by making sure that statements are supported with facts.
- Investigate the truth and accuracy of information rather than automatically accepting it as true.
- Question the validity of statements and information.
  Determine whether they correspond with reality by asking:
  - How does the speaker know this to be true?
  - Are there any facts that disprove the statement or information?
  - How reliable are the sources of information?
  - How can I test the validity of the statement or information?

Be Open-Minded

- Seeing the world only from your perspective or point of view can hinder your ability to think critically. This inflexibility can be frustrating for you and other people.
- Take time to listen to others, even if your first impulse is to say "no."
- Seeing beyond your perspective can be difficult, but can open up new ways of thinking about things and also open lines of communication.
- Hear others' opinions, even if they're not your own. You may agree or you may not.
- Show empathy by putting yourself in other peoples' shoes to see from their point of view.
  Ask questions such as these:
  - What is similar and dissimilar about the other person's beliefs?
  - What about the person's beliefs are of value to me and other people?
  - What can I learn from this different perspective?

Think Analytically

- Recognize when statements need the support of evidence.
- Evaluate the pros and cons of adopting another point of view that is contrary to your current point of view.
- Take time to understand an idea before accepting, rejecting or modifying it.
- Break your tasks and your goals into small tasks.
- Analyze a problem before you try to solve it.

SECTION VI

MENTAL SHARPNESS

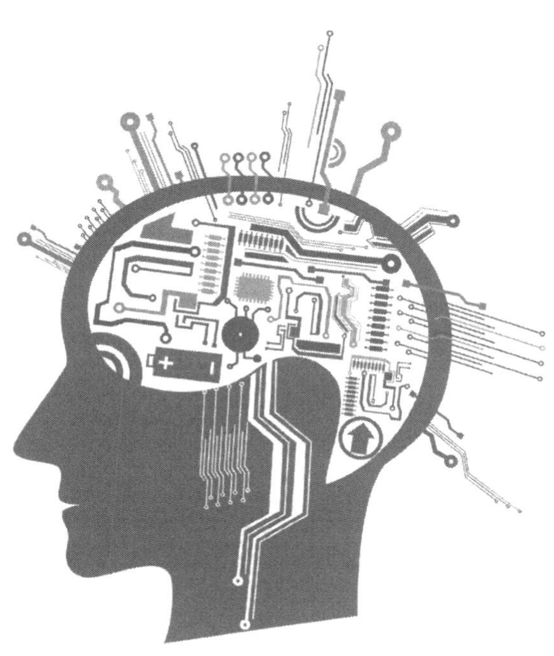

Mental acuity was never born from comfortable circumstances.

– Haruki Murakami

Name ______________________________

Date ______________________________

MENTAL SHARPNESS

Step 1: Self-Assessment Introduction and Directions

Mental sharpness does not mean how smart you are. Instead, it is ability to do the following:

- remember
- focus
- concentrate
- use common sense
- make good decisions

The *Mental Sharpness Self-Assessment* is designed to help you become aware of your own mental sharpness. It contains three individual scales. Read each statement carefully. Circle the number of the response under the column True, Somewhat True or Not True that shows how descriptive each statement is of you.

Do not pay attention to the numbers, just the headings:

- True
- Somewhat True
- Not True

In the following example, the circled 2 indicates that the statement is Somewhat True about the person completing the scale.

	TRUE	SOMEWHAT TRUE	NOT TRUE
When concentrating ...			
I have trouble focusing my mind on tasks.	1	(2)	3

This is not a test and there are no right or wrong answers. Do not spend too much time thinking about your answers. Your initial response will be the most true for you. Be sure to respond to every statement.

Turn the page and complete the Self-Assessment

MENTAL SHARPNESS

Step 1: Self-Assessment Scales

	TRUE	SOMEWHAT TRUE	NOT TRUE
When concentrating ...			
I have trouble focusing my mind on tasks	1	2	3
I get distracted easily	1	2	3
I can maintain focus on a single task for long spans of time	3	2	1
I can concentrate even when I'm tired	3	2	1
I get easily distracted when working on a task	1	2	3
I am self-disciplined in my concentration	3	2	1
I have irrelevant information constantly popping into my head	1	2	3
My mind does not drift away when concentrating	3	2	1

C. TOTAL = ________

	TRUE	SOMEWHAT TRUE	NOT TRUE
When it comes to my memory...			
I forget where I put my keys/glasses/cell phone	1	2	3
I do not forget anniversaries or birthdays	3	2	1
I am not able to remember people and their names	1	2	3
I do not have trouble recognizing people's faces	3	2	1
I remember to pay my bills on time	3	2	1
I often forget why I have gone into a room	1	2	3
I forget the times of my appointments	1	2	3
I forget my technology passwords	1	2	3

M. TOTAL = ________

	TRUE	SOMEWHAT TRUE	NOT TRUE
When it comes to my judgment ...			
I have trouble making choices	1	2	3
I show good judgment	3	2	1
I behave in socially inappropriate ways	1	2	3
I make poor financial decisions	1	2	3
I wear clothes that are appropriate for people my age	3	2	1
I have good common sense	3	2	1
I do not evaluate evidence carefully to make good decisions	1	2	3
I form opinions wisely and objectively	3	2	1

D. TOTAL = ________

Go to the Scoring Directions on the next page

MENTAL SHARPNESS

Step 1: Scale Scoring Directions

By being aware of your mental sharpness, you will be able to expand it even more. On the previous page, total the circles in each scale and write them on the line marked TOTAL. Then transfer that number below. Next, add your three scale scores below to get your Mental Sharpness Self-Assessment total score.

C. Concentration Scale TOTAL = ______

M. Memory Scale TOTAL = ______

D. Decisions Scale TOTAL = ______

***Mental Sharpness Self-Assessment* total score** = ______

Profile Interpretation

Total Individual Scales Scores	Total Self-Assessment Score	Result	Indications
Scores from 19 to 24	57 to 72	High	If you score in the high range, you tend to have limited problems with your mental sharpness. The activities will help you to maintain your mental sharpness.
Scores from 14 to 18	40 to 56	Moderate	If you score in the moderate range, you tend to have some problems with your mental sharpness. The activities will help you enhance your mental sharpness.
Scores from 8 to 13	24 to 39	Low	If you score in the low range, you tend to have problems with your mental sharpness. The activities will help you to increase your mental sharpness.

Regardless of your score on the individual scales or the total self-assessment, all of the exercises that follow have been designed to help you develop openness to new ideas.

Go to the Scale Descriptions on the next page

MENTAL SHARPNESS

Step 1: Scale Descriptions

The **Concentration Scale** indicates the level of your ability to focus your mind on a task or series of tasks while ignoring any distractions in your environment.

The **Memory Scale** indicates the level of your ability to remember and recall information, people, places, and events from the past. It is your ability to retrieve information from a short time ago (short-term memory) or a long time ago (long-term memory).

The **Decisions Scale** indicates the level of your ability to judge, make decisions and form opinions wisely and objectively. It is your ability to show discernment and good sense.

Step 2: Recognize and Develop a Support System

Some people are better than others at accepting your change in mental acuity. You will want to have these people as part of your support system to help you in your efforts to think more sharply. Identify those people in your life who will support you and ask them if they would be willing to support you in your efforts to grow in this area. Complete the following table with people who might be able to support you with your efforts to think more sharply.

Supporter	How This Person Can Support Me	How I Can Contact This Person
My mom	*By giving me someone I trust to talk to when I need help*	*Phone 000-000-0000*

Keep this list handy. Call, email or text when you need support.

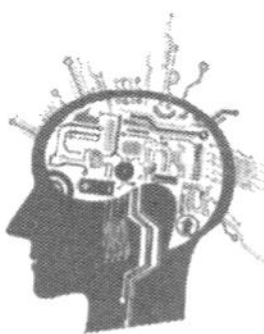

MENTAL SHARPNESS

Step 3: Keep a Journal – My Mental Sharpness

The lack of being sharp mentally is a problem that many people, young and old, have in their life. The following journaling questions will help you explore your mental sharpness.

When do you have the most trouble concentrating? Explain.

___

___

What can you do to help yourself concentrate better?

___

___

What do you remember easily? Explain.

___

___

What do you have the most trouble remembering?

___

___

What do you think you could do to help yourself remember better?

___

___

What decisions are difficult to make? Explain.

___

___

Who helps you make those decisions?

___

___

Who else could help you make good decisions?

___

___

MENTAL SHARPNESS

Step 4: Set Goals

People who have trouble - focusing their attention and concentrating on important tasks; remembering people, places and things; using good common sense; making effective decisions – can develop goals to help themselves attain and maintain mental sharpness. Well-conceived action plans can help you stay motivated as you work toward your goals. For your action plan, identify the behavior you want to change and specific goals, or smaller goals required to reach your ultimate goals for improving mental sharpness.

The behavior I want to change ______________________________

Goals need to be SMART:

Specific, **M**easureable, **A**ttainable, **R**ealistic and **T**ime-Specific

Goals	How I Will Measure Each Goal	How Each Goal Is Attainable and Realistic	Time Deadline	How This Change Will Help Me
To focus on what people are saying and not get distracted.	*If, when I walk away, I remember what they say.*	*If I don't look at my watch or the people who are walking by, I'll retain what is said.*	*My birthday*	*I will feel confident because I paid attention and will remember people's comments.*

If you are having trouble identifying goals, consult TIPS, page 104.

MENTAL SHARPNESS

Step 5: Monitor My Behavior – Concentration

Your ability to concentrate is critical in your forming and maintaining effective thinking patterns. Set some goals that will help you to be more realistic in concentrating when you need to. The chart below will help you to keep track of your progress. Keeping track of your behaviors through logs will help you know when you are making positive changes in your behavior. Periodically re-evaluate your successes and setbacks. Once you reach your goal(s), set new ones to improve or maintain what you have already achieved. Use a separate page for each change.

EXAMPLE:

My "concentration" behavior change *Begin questioning what people say about which foods are health y*

My goal *Learn a better system for critically examining information*

Date	My Accomplishment	How It Felt
1/1/2014	*I focused on my child's ballgame and was able to talk about details on the way home.*	*I felt much calmer throughout the day.*

Concentration

My "concentration" behavior change________________________

My goal________________________

Date	My Accomplishment	How It Felt

(Continued on the next page)

MENTAL SHARPNESS

Step 5: Monitor My Behavior – Concentration *(Continued)*

Complete the two tables below to learn more about your ability to concentrate.

Situations When I DO NOT Focus and/or Concentrate	Why I DO NOT Focus and/or Concentrate in These Situations	How I Feel When I DO NOT Focus and/or Concentrate

Situations When I DO Focus and/or Concentrate	Why I DO Focus and/or Concentrate in These Situations	How I Feel When I DO Focus and/or Concentrate

MENTAL SHARPNESS

Step 5: Monitor My Behavior – Memory

To be intellectually sharp, you need to continue to develop your memory. Your ability to remember things, people, and events is important in your overall wellness. Personal wellness is fairly easy to track. Through the chart below, you will monitor your progress toward being able to enhance your memory. Re-evaluate your goals as you develop more confidence in this process. Once you reach your goal(s), set new ones to improve or maintain what you have already achieved. Use a separate page for each change.

EXAMPLE:

My "memory" behavior change *I want to acknowledge my loved ones' birthdays*

My goal *To learn tools and techniques to remember things that are important to me*

Date	My Accomplishment	How It Felt
1/1/2014	*I sent my grandson's birthday card on time!*	*It felt wonderful.*

Memory

My "memory" behavior change____

My goal ____

Date	My Accomplishment	How It Felt

(Continued on the next page)

MENTAL SHARPNESS

Step 5: Monitoring My Behavior – Memory *(Continued)*

Fill in the two tables below to learn more about your memory.

Things I Easily Remember	Why I Am Able to Remember So Easily	How I Feel About it When I Remember

Things I Just DO NOT Remember	Why I DO NOT Remember These Things	What I Can Do to Remember

MENTAL SHARPNESS

Step 5: Monitor My Behavior – Decisions

Intellectually well people are able to make good decisions and positive judgments. They have good common sense and are able to act in socially appropriate ways. Monitoring your progress toward your goals of enhancing your sense of sound judgment is important in your overall wellness. Periodic re-evaluations promote your success. Once you reach your goal(s), set new ones to improve or maintain what you have already achieved. Use a separate page for each change.

EXAMPLE:

My "decision-making" behavior change *Be a better decision maker*

My goal *Evaluate the pros and cons of decisions I need to make*

Date	My Accomplishment	How It Felt
1/1/2014	*I made a decision to visit my parents even though I was angry about something.*	*I felt excited that I was going to see them and decided how to discuss my feelings tactfully.*

Decisions

My "decision-making" behavior change ____________________

My goal ____________________

Date	My Accomplishment	How It Felt

(Continued on the next page)

MENTAL SHARPNESS

Step 5: Monitor My Behavior – Decisions *(Continued)*

Complete the two tables below to learn more about decisions you have made.

Great Decisions I Have Made	Why I Was Able to Do So	How I Made the Decisions

Poor Decisions I Have Made	How and Why I Made These Decisions	How I Can Make Better Decisions in Similar Situations

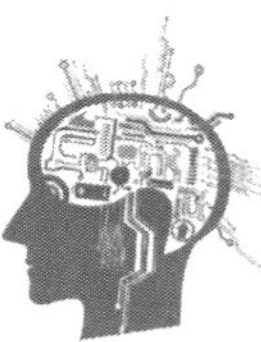

MENTAL SHARPNESS

Step 6: Reward Myself

People who exhibit intellectual sharpness are able to focus and concentrate well, have sufficient memory, make good decisions, and display sound judgments. When you are able to exhibit these skills, remember to reward yourself! This will motivate you to duplicate this behavior more. The challenge is to decide what reward would motivate you to reach your goal. Your reward needs to be something that will give you the incentive to achieve your goals. It needs to be within your budget and something you'll be excited about. If you are buying yourself something, be sure your reward is something you wouldn't ordinarily buy or do. **Brainstorm some possible rewards.**

- Rewards that would be meaningful to me ______________________
- Small rewards I could give myself ______________________
- Large rewards I could give myself ______________________
- Things that would not cost money and would be fun ______________________
- Rewards that I can afford and that would be fun ______________________
- Rewards that I enjoy alone ______________________
- Rewards I enjoy with people who support me ______________________

You deserve a pat on the back for the hard work you are completing in this section. Rewards help you to pay attention to your triumphs, not your setbacks. Rewards will create good feelings and propel you to want to work harder to reach your goals. Whenever you have completed or achieved one of your goals, treat yourself to one of the items on your list.

You can also reward yourself by giving yourself positive affirmations when you have achieved a goal. Below are some samples. Cut them out and post them in visible spots at home and work! If these don't work for your goal, write your own on sticky notes!

I will get rid of my mental clutter.	*I have a great memory.*	I will take time to make careful decisions.
My judgment is sound.	*I am working to develop my sense of mental clarity.*	I can remember things easily.
Concentration is critical in my life.	**I have sound judgment.**	*I take my time to work out complicated problems.*

"I'm getting so absent-minded and forgetful. Sometimes in the middle of a sentence, I . . . "

~ Milton Berle

Does this happen to you? ________ What do you do when it happens? ______________________

____

MENTAL SHARPNESS

Step 7: Tips For Motivated Behavior Modification

Concentration

- Don't let other people or other events distract you when you are focusing.
- Stay engaged in mental pursuits that will be interesting to you. Learn a second language, take a class or join a discussion group.
- Learn how to be more in the *here and now*, and fully present, rather than having your mind fleeting here and there.
- Remove surrounding distraction. Turn off your cell phone, shut down your computer, etc.
- Set specific production goals for yourself to achieve.

Memory

- Make information meaningful to you, to be able to remember it more easily.
- Use your body. Remember that people remember 90% of what they do. Therefore, see the information, repeat it to yourself and then use your body to remember it.
- Create pictures, draw diagrams, or make cartoons to recall abstract concepts.
- Recite, write, and repeat information multiple times (out loud) to place it into your memory.
- Keep your mind active: read, play different types of games (cards, board, crossword, Sudoku, computer), exercise, sleep enough but not too much, have fun, socialize, be organized, laugh!

Decisions

- Learn from experiences. Make a mental or written note of the key learning points, so that you may draw on these experiences in the future.
- Develop ideas clearly, focus intently, think hard, ask for support if needed, and be able to commit to something after thoughtful deliberation.
- Know when to get help, seek out more knowledgeable people, and find resources to gain more insight and tools to help you deal with the obstacles you face.
- Be able to balance the risks/cons and the benefits/pros before making each decision.
- Know you are always willing to learn new ways to look at issues from different points of view; listen to feedback, criticisms, and others' perspectives.

SECTION VII

INDEPENDENT THINKING

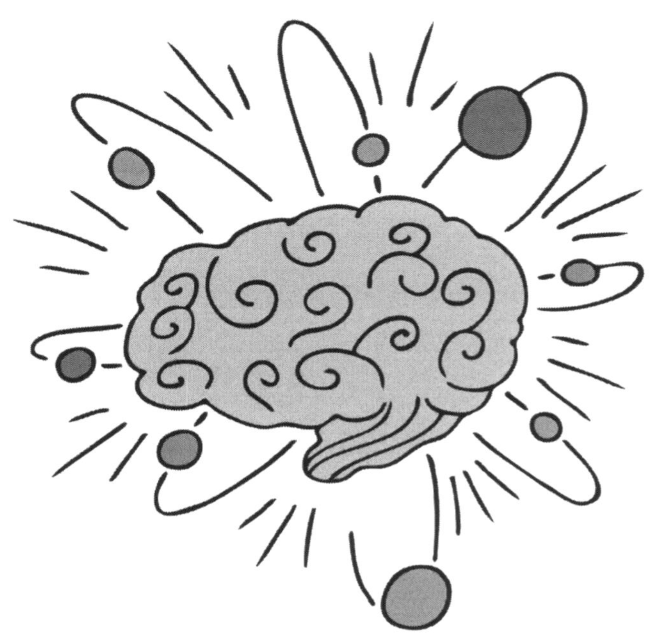

People can tell you to keep your mouth shut,
but that doesn't stop you from
having your own opinion.

– Anne Frank

Name ______________________________

Date ______________________________

INDEPENDENT THINKING

Step 1: Self-Assessment Introduction and Directions

The *Independent Thinking Self-Assessment* will help you identify how independent you are in making decisions about your life. This self-assessment contains three individual scales. Read each of the statements carefully and decide whether or not the statement describes you. If the statement does describe you, circle the YES next to that item. If the statement does not describe you, circle the NO next to that item.

In the following example, the circled "No" indicates the statement is NOT descriptive of the person completing the scales.

I follow my conscience in making decisions . . . . YES 

This is not a test and there are no right or wrong answers. Do not spend too much time thinking about your answers. Your initial response will be the most true for you. Be sure to respond to every statement.

Turn to the next page and complete the Self-Assessment

INDEPENDENT THINKING

Step 1: Self-Assessment Scales

I follow my conscience in making decisions	YES	NO
I often question information if I'm not sure	YES	NO
I speak up when those in authority are wrong	YES	NO
I am often skeptical of what people in authority say	YES	NO
I try not to accept without question whatever I'm taught	YES	NO
I sometimes go along with the thoughts of others, but only if I agree with them	YES	NO
I will gladly share ideas that are different from others' ideas	YES	NO
I evaluate evidence to support claims rather than blindly agree with others' claims	YES	NO
I rarely defer to others – I would rather rely on my own judgment	YES	NO
I question whether information really makes sense or not	YES	NO

1 TOTAL ________

I make my own independent decisions	YES	NO
I do not rely on others to make decisions for me	YES	NO
I do not like it when others make decisions for me	YES	NO
I think through information and then make my own decisions	YES	NO
I ask others for their opinion, but make my own decisions	YES	NO
I go along with the decision made by groups if I agree	YES	NO
I make decisions based on my code of values and morals	YES	NO
I consider what really matters to me before making decisions	YES	NO
I use an effective decision-making process	YES	NO
I don't make excuses for poor decisions	YES	NO

2 TOTAL = ________

I say what I think in an honest, open and direct way	YES	NO
I assert myself if I think I'm right	YES	NO
I express my needs and wants	YES	NO
I believe I have the right to express myself	YES	NO
I listen to others, but I do not always go along with them	YES	NO
I will not blindly do what others want or expect	YES	NO
I express my opinions even if others don't agree with me	YES	NO
I can express feedback to others constructively	YES	NO
I am respectful and listen to others, even if I don't agree	YES	NO
I have the right to protest unfair treatment or criticism	YES	NO

3 TOTAL = ________

Go to the Scoring Directions on the next page

INDEPENDENT THINKING

Step 1: Self-Assessment Scoring Directions

The *Independent Thinking Self-Assessment* is designed to measure how you think for yourself. On the previous page, total the YES circles in each scale and write them on the line marked TOTAL. Then transfer that score below. Next, add your three scores to get your Independent Thinking Self-Assessment total score.

1 Question Authority Scale TOTAL = ________

2 Make Decisions Scale TOTAL = ________

3 Assert Yourself Scale TOTAL = ________

***Creative Thinking Self-Assessment* total score** ________

Profile Interpretation

Individual Scales Scores	Total Self-Assessment Score	Result	Indications
Scores from 7 to 10	Scores from 21 to 30	High	You have definitely developed the ability to think independently. The activities that follow will help you develop even greater skills in this area.
Scores from 4 to 6	Scores from 11 to 20	Moderate	You have developed some of the ability to think independently. The activities that follow will help you develop even greater skills in this area.
Scores from 0 to 3	Scores from 0 to 10	Low	You have quite a way to go to start thinking independently. The activities that follow will help you develop skills in this area.

Go to the Scale Descriptions on the next page

INDEPENDENT THINKING

Step 1: Scale Descriptions

Question Authority – People scoring high on this scale tend to follow their conscience when making decisions. They question what others say, evaluate evidence rather than blindly believing, and speak up respectfully if they believe others (even those in authority) are wrong.

Make Decisions – People scoring high on this scale tend to make their own independent decisions. They do not want to rely on others to make their decisions and are effective decision makers. They listen to others' opinions and then make their own independent decisions.

Assert Yourself – People scoring high on this scale tend to be assertive in an honest, open and direct way when they believe they are correct. They express feedback to others in a constructive manner and give their opinions without the fear of being wrong or looked down upon. They express their needs directly and honestly, and they will not blindly do what others expect.

Step 2: Recognize and Develop a Support System

Often, people think they need help in assertively stating what they need and desire. Good, trusted friends and family can be helpful. Think about who can help you to be more assertive and how. Not every supportive person in your life will fit this bill; so now is the time to identify those who can support you in your efforts to grow and how they can help you. Different people can be supportive in different ways. Complete the following table with people who might support you in making smart, assertive decisions in your life.

Supporter	How This Person Can Support Me	How I Can Contact This Person
My friend who has no problem being assertive	*She can keep reminding me that I have rights, too*	*Phone or text 000-0000* *email Friend@xyz.com*

Keep this list handy. Call, email or text when you need support.

INDEPENDENT THINKING

Step 3: Keep a Journal – Making Decisions

Anyone can develop independent thinking and decision-making skills. The following journaling questions are designed to help you think carefully about how you make decisions. Answer them honestly to help you have insight into your decision-making process.

How do you make decisions? Explain.

(Impulsively, ask others, alone, instinctively, procrastinate, etc.)

What are the positive aspects of your decision-making system?

What are the negative aspects of your decision-making system?

To whom do you listen when you are making decisions? Explain the outcomes.

Whom do you allow to make decisions for you? Explain the outcomes.

How can you be more assertive in making your own decisions?

INDEPENDENT THINKING

Step 4: Set Goals

The next step in thinking more independently and making good decisions is to set specific goals that will allow you to be an independent decision maker. The action plan that follows will help you to achieve your goals by keeping you motivated. For your action plan, first identify the behaviors that will enhance your decision-making skills. Then set specific goals, or smaller goals that can help keep you motivated until you reach your goals of living more independently.

The behavior I want to change ____

Goals need to be SMART:

Specific, **M**easureable, **A**ttainable, **R**ealistic and **T**ime-Specific

Goals	How I Will Measure Each Goal	How Each Goal Is Attainable and Realistic	Time Deadline	How This Change Will Help Me
I will not make my decision based on what my partner says we are doing.	*I will hear my partner's opinion but think for myself and give my opinion.*	*If I can explain to my partner that I want to be a part of the decision making.*	*Immediately*	*I will be more accepting of OUR decisions.*

If you are having trouble identifying goals, consult TIPS, page 118.

INDEPENDENT THINKING

Step 5: Monitor My Behavior – Question Authority

Do you believe everything that people tell you? Do you question what they say? Do you research? In the table below, identify some of the goals you have that will encourage you to do more independent thinking. Monitor your progress toward your goals by keeping track of your behaviors below. Periodic re-evaluations support your success. Once you reach your goal(s), set new ones to improve or maintain what you have already achieved. Use a separate page for each change.

EXAMPLE:

My "questioning authority" behavior change *I will search for facts to back up claims*

My goal *I need to stop believing everything a salesperson tells me about their product*

Date	My Accomplishment	How It Felt
1/1/2014	*I chose a car based on research and factual information.*	*I like my car and I am proud of myself.*

Question Authority

My "questioning authority" behavior change ____________________

My goal ____________________

Date	My Accomplishment	How It Felt

(Continued on the next page)

INDEPENDENT THINKING

Step 5: Monitor My Behavior – Make Decisions

It is important to learn to make your own informed decisions. This will allow you to take responsibility for your own life and stop relying on others. This is something that you can track fairly easily during your week. In the chart that follows, monitor your progress in decision-making. Keeping track will help you follow your progress. Periodic re-evaluations are vital for your success in your developing effective decision-making skills. Once you reach your goal(s), set new ones to improve or maintain what you have already achieved. Use a separate page for each change.

EXAMPLE:

My "decision-making" behavior change *To make my own decisions for which job to apply.*

My goal *To listen to others but follow my own passion.*

Date	My Accomplishment	How It Felt
1/1/2014	*I asked friends what they thought I'd be suited for and why. Then made my decision based on their comments but particularly on my passion.*	*Fulfilling*

Make Decisions

My "decision-making" behavior change______________________________________

My goal____

Date	My Accomplishment	How It Felt

(Continued on the next page)

INDEPENDENT THINKING

Step 5: Monitor My Behavior – Assert Yourself

To express your own thoughts regardless of what others say, to express what you want and need, and to give your opinions in an assertive way, without being passive or aggressive. Sounds easy, doesn't it? In reality, doing this is not always easy. Use the table below to set assertiveness goals. Keeping track of your behaviors will help you monitor your progress. Once you reach your goal(s), set new ones to improve or maintain what you have already achieved. Use a separate page for each change.

EXAMPLE:

My "assertiveness" behavior change *To express my opinion in meetings at work in an open, honest and direct way.*

My goal *To be seen as a serious candidate for the supervisor's job.*

Date	My Accomplishment	How It Felt
1/1/2014	*I gave my opinion at a meeting and most everyone agreed. I responded in an assertive way when someone challenged me.*	*I felt proud of myself.*

Assert Yourself

My "assertiveness" behavior change ______________________

My goal ______________________

Date	My Accomplishment	How It Felt

(Continued on the next page)

INDEPENDENT THINKING

Step 5: Monitoring My Behavior – Journal Processing

QUESTION AUTHORITY

What authorities (or people who seem to know what they are talking about) do you question? How do you evaluate what they say?

Describe a situation in which you spoke up when you thought someone was wrong. How did it turn out?

Why did it turn out that way?

MAKE DECISIONS

What is the decision-making process you use? When has it been effective? When has it been ineffective?

Why has it been ineffective?

What types of decisions do you tend to let others make for you? How do these work out?

ASSERT YOURSELF

In what situations are you most assertive? In which ones are you not?

Why not?

When you are not assertive, are you passive or aggressive? Explain.

INDEPENDENT THINKING

Step 6: Reward Myself

Making your own decisions works well when you are open to other's opinions, willing to question what people say in an assertive way, and then, make up your own mind. Here is another decision. What reward would motivate you to reach your decision goal? Your reward needs to be something that will give you the incentive to achieve your goals. It needs to be within your budget and something you'll be excited about. If you are buying yourself something, be sure your reward is something you wouldn't ordinarily buy or do. **Brainstorm some possible rewards.**

- Rewards that would be meaningful to me ____________________
- Small rewards I could give myself ____________________
- Large rewards I could give myself ____________________
- Things that would not cost money and would be fun ____________________
- Rewards that I can afford and that would be fun ____________________
- Rewards that I enjoy alone ____________________
- Rewards I enjoy with people who support me ____________________

You deserve a pat on the back for the hard work you are completing in this section. Rewards help you to pay attention to your triumphs, not your setbacks. Rewards will create good feelings and propel you to want to work harder to reach your goals. Whenever you have completed or achieved one of your goals, treat yourself to one of the items on your list.

You can also reward yourself by giving yourself positive affirmations when you have achieved a goal. Below are some samples. Cut them out and post them in visible spots at home and work! If these don't work for your goal, write your own on sticky notes!

I don't worry about what others say.	***I will express myself assertively.***	I can make light of difficult situations.
My own decisions are right for me.	*I have the right to question what people suggest to me.*	I am true to myself.
I am an independent thinker.	**I don't worry about the judgment of others.**	*I am able to share ideas that are different from others.*

Emancipate yourselves from mental slavery. None but ourselves can free our minds.
~ Bob Marley

What does this quotation mean to you? ____________________

____

INDEPENDENT THINKING

Step 7: Tips For Motivated Behavior Modification

Question Authority

- Realize that those who act like experts may not be experts after all.
- Research and evaluate the statements of others to be sure they are indeed factual.
- Distinguish when the experts are providing you with facts versus simply providing you with their opinions.
- Watch for referenced qualifiers such as all, none, never, often, always, and many.
- Take it upon yourself to explore the examples or facts that provide evidence of truth.

Make Decisions

- Remember that your decisions are choices you can make, not for others to make.
- Listen to others. Brainstorm ideas. Then, make up your own mind.
- Think critically about all of the possible choices and decide which one will work best for you given your situation.
- Identify the level of the decision to be made. Is it a small decision or a large one? This distinction will help you decide the extent of your resources to dedicate to the decision.
- Make a decision that is logical and well thought out. Ask others for their opinions, but make the decision yourself.

Assert Yourself

- Feel free to speak, in an open, honest and direct way. Say what you honestly believe.
- If others do not agree with you, respond in the same open, honest and direct way.
- You do not need to go along with the crowd. If you believe something different from the crowd, assertively express your thoughts and stick to them.
- Do not worry about your opinions being wrong. Express them anyway. They are your opinions, and others can agree or disagree. That's okay.
- When you express your opinions and someone does not agree, do not react in a negative way. They, like you, are entitled to their opinion.
- You have the right to express yourself.